Beyond the Breed

the new way to know and understand your dog

HEATHER STEVENS

Beyond the Breed

ISBN 978-1-914209-02-4

eISBN 978-1-914209-03-1

Published in 2021 by Flying Squad Books

© Heather Stevens 2021

Contents

For Sparky, the German Shepherd dog that started my dog journey, and to the many that followed with gifts of learning, understanding and love. Thank you. I miss you still.

Foreword
by Dr Isla Fishburn BSc., PhD

I remember when I first came across the term 'functional character'. Sitting at my desk in what was then known as the BIOME lab at the University of Sheffield, I was head deep in working through my PhD thesis. I was reading all I could about wolves as I had my mind set on a postdoctoral or research position that explored wolf ecology, conservation and coexistence. At the time, little did I know that I was destined for other canine-related duties; but I am so grateful that this, indeed, was the path laid out before me.

I first came across functional characters after discovering the writings of a wolf biologist called Dr Gordon Haber. Haber had studied various wolf packs of Alaska, specifically those of Denali National Park, for over 40 years. In his work, Haber discussed countless observations of how individual wolves in a certain group appeared to have a particular functional purpose or role within that group. He called this functional character. I guess you can say it was almost like a job that a wolf would hold for the support, functioning and enhanced survival of its group. I found this fascinating, as I had already been reading about social structure and dynamics of social group animals – from insects to mammals. Just like ants have a social structure that complements the survival of the group – whereby there are different duties for the ant colony to live and survive – large social mammals, such as many canids, have similar social structures that benefit the group as a whole.

I was hooked. I already held an admiration for and fascination with wolves, but to learn of functional characters and that a given wolf group would have a mix of these to complement and support each and every one in that group ignited an even deeper desire and drive to explore more. I had managed to pick up a few functional character descriptions from Haber's writings, as well as some other scientific papers and books I was reading on the subject of social roles in socially living animals. At the time, I also had a wolf dog and it made me wonder, 'Do dogs have functional characters too?' I explored more.

I began to study more about Haber's work. Unfortunately, Haber died in a tragic plane accident in 2009, when he was conducting further wolf research. Fortunately, the incredible work of Haber and his sheer determination to share the inner life of wolves can be easily accessed for all to view in his field notes, journals, reports and accounts by visiting www.alaskawolves.org. His work has also been compiled into one of my favourite books on wolf biology, ecology, conservation and life, *Among Wolves: Gordon Haber's Insights into Alaska's Most Misunderstood Animal*, edited by Marybeth Holleman.

As luck would have it, while I was exploring research options after my PhD, I was presented with an opportunity to study and work with captive wolves at a wildlife park in the UK. I jumped at the chance. Being able to observe, study and sit with relatively undisturbed wolves even in captivity allowed me to see functional characters in action – and I did! I would spend much of my day quietly observing one of the bigger groups of wolves that were in my care. I never really expected my passion for wolf behaviour, ecology and conservation to move over into a passion for domestic dogs. But with my own wolf dog and love of dogs since a child, I began to explore the relevance of not only functional character and how it applies to dogs but how my knowledge of ecosystem health, ecology, cellular communication and conservation applied to domestic animals like dogs.

As a zoologist and conservation biologist, I made the decision to live with a dog, as I wanted to experience what it was like to coexist with another species. With all my knowledge I felt equipped to appreciate the physical needs of an animal, as well as the spiritual needs of a living soul. While I have always followed a path that follows earth-based teachings, it was during my PhD that I began to purposefully align the wisdom of indigenous teachings with science and continue to do so to this day. I never once saw my dog as 'just a dog' or that it had to do or be what I wanted. I saw the life I have with my dog as a partnership, a relationship, and one of equality. I wanted to know all I could so my dog could have her best life, which I continue to explore, research and learn to this day. I assumed that everyone who decides to live with another animal has the same level of exploration, teaching, understanding and desire to learn all they can about the animal they chose to live with. I quickly learned this isn't necessarily the case and, because I care about life for all, I created teachings around canine wellness that combine science with indigenous wisdom to better the life of dogs, their guardians and, hopefully, all life.

That's when I met Heather! I was a speaker at a conference all about natural dog care and I was talking about what we can learn about wolves to help us improve our understanding of dogs. This talk included a section on functional characters. Not only was I hooked on this subject, but there and then, I also got Heather hooked on it too, and a few others also. Since then, many others that have listened to my teachings are also hooked on this subject – I am certain that after reading *Beyond the Breed* you will be too!

Heather has been a dog behaviourist and trainer for many years and runs a well-established dog crèche. She knows a lot about dogs and has a long list of credentials and experience. She wanted to know more about functional character and how this could benefit individual dogs she works with, as well as how this may fit in with her dog crèche. Heather has excelled at applying the subject and teachings of functional characters in her work, going even further and holding functional character workshops for others to learn about this important subject for the benefit of a dog's happiness, life and behaviour.

That wasn't enough for Heather. She wanted to take her teachings, experience and knowledge of functional characters even further so that she could bring these teachings to an even wider audience. One day, I received a message from Heather: 'Hey Isla – I'm going to write a book on functional characters and make a difference to the life of dogs. What do you think?'

Heather already had it in the bag – she could already see the layout of the book, how she could include personal experience from not only her own dogs, but those of her clients as well as the functional character workshops she holds and the dogs at her crèche. I love Heather's functional character workshops – they bring this subject to life and clearly show functional characters in action! Everyone who attends her workshops gets as hooked on functional characters as Heather and myself already are.

But, for those of you who want more or who have not had the privilege yet of attending a workshop, Heather has excelled again and brought functional characters to your home through *Beyond the Breed*. The book is filled with such useful and helpful information, stretching you literally beyond the breed that your dog is. Every dog is an individual and dogs have individual functional characters that can help explain their behaviour, likes, dislikes, social interaction, diet choices, conflict, learning and so much more. From my perspective, we are denying a dog the opportunity to be fully understood and seen when we do not consider functional character. Now you can learn about this subject and how it applies to your dog in *Beyond the Breed*!

It is my hope that eventually we all return to a place of coherence, where we have acceptance, understanding and respect for all of life and all living beings. That is certainly one thing that our dogs are here to teach us – as we explore and learn more and more about how to make life better for dogs, this has to include making life better for ourselves. When we make life better for ourselves, we reach a more balanced and aligned connection with all things.

Heather provides you with just that – an opportunity to learn something about your dog that you perhaps did not know about. What is your dog's functional character, and how does this help you understand your dog better and what s/he needs? Have fun seeing your dog beyond being just a dog and beyond just a breed!

Dr Isla Fishburn
Founder of Kachina Canine and Sacred Creator
Canine wellness advisor, behaviourist
and shamanic practitioner

Introduction

In 1962, my family and a friend of my parents moved from Hertfordshire to the south coast in West Sussex. Between them they had bought a petrol station that also had a café and some B&B rooms. For nearly two years, the three of them busied themselves with building the business, which was well placed for passing traffic between the Surrey suburbs and the seaside. It was exciting as a child, and I was thrilled to have a puppy as part of our new life. He was a German Shepherd dog, known as an Alsatian in those days, and we named him Sparky.

My parents were always terribly busy – my mother running the whole thing, and my father mending cars for people. I would fetch spanners for him and hold the nuts and bolts that he removed from an engine. My sister preferred to play with dolls, so I spent a lot of time playing with Sparky. He became my world, but little did I realise the devastation that lay ahead.

In the early hours of a cold October morning in 1964, Sparky went into my parents' bedroom whimpering. My father told him to be quiet but Sparky persisted. He then realised that he could smell smoke. We escaped with our lives but lost everything. A while later, the family friend moved back to London and took Sparky with him. And a short time after that, my father walked out on us. So, before I reached double digits in age, I had lost my home, my dog and my father.

However, what I gained in that short time was a lifelong affinity with dogs. Sparky was the catalyst. Thanks to him and hundreds of other dogs that have crossed my path in the past half-century, here we are at *Beyond the Breed*. There is, however, another crucial 'ingredient' in the making of this book – my dear friend Dr Isla Fishburn BSc., PhD.

I am deeply grateful to Rachel Bean RVN for introducing me to this amazing lady at the Natural Dog Conference in Birmingham in 2015. Isla is a canine wellness practitioner, conservation biologist, shamanic practitioner and wolf specialist who runs Kachina Canine in Northumberland, England. After she introduced me to functional characters, I quickly became as obsessed as Dr Isla with this aspect of dogs.

It became apparent that an understanding of a dog's functional character made the chances of resolving, and preventing, behaviour problems such as aggression much better. Of course, there are other things to be considered, but the functional characters concept explains so much. It explains why dogs vary in their responses to different environments and situations, people and other dogs. How quickly they bounce back from something that startles them is a lot to do with their functional character. In all the years I have worked with dogs, and all the courses, seminars and lectures I have attended, learning about functional characters has been the most significant and enlightening piece of knowledge so far.

A dog's functional character determines its function within a social group and is set at birth. Functional characters are not breed dependent. For example, some Border Collies are smart, while others need constant repetition to learn even the simplest exercise. And some crossbreeds can knock your socks off with their capacity to learn and execute long behaviour chains. This is functional characters in action – it's not just about the breed!

In addition to my behaviour reformation work, I run a busy daycare facility for dogs, which allows me to study functional characters in action, all day every day, which is awesome! This knowledge is passed on to dog owners through our regular workshops, and at behaviour consultations.

This book aims to provide a deeper understanding of functional characters and help you determine the functional character of your current pet(s). If you are currently thinking about getting another dog or puppy, this book may provide you with an insight as to which functional character(s) would be best suited to you, your lifestyle and your current dog(s).

Some canine communication is so subtle, and I believe dogs have always paid a high price for our lack of awareness and understanding. They do or 'say' something because they are a dog – we don't understand it and, before you know it, off goes another pet to a rescue centre or over Rainbow Bridge. We must become more aware of our dogs at a deeper level, and as an ecosystem. We must continue to enhance our knowledge of how they communicate and their numerous communication methods. For example, did you ever stop to think about how a puppy's tail displays its functional character while the litter is eating?

Also, I hope that a perception of canine functional characters may help stem the continual rise of aggression. Understanding how the different characters interact and communicate would prevent much of the dog–dog aggression that so many behaviour specialists see.

With so many of us owning multiple dogs these days, it would be great to 'read' their interactions more clearly. What if you had a way to choose your next addition in a way that you could be 99% sure of them fitting in with your existing group? The knowledge of functional characters enables us to tailor socialising and training in a way that we have never been able to before.

Knowledge of the characters is a considerable benefit to breeders. It has already helped many of them identify which individuals they particularly want to breed from and those they do not. It also helps determine which individuals are best suited to assistance dog duties, obedience and other competition fun, or protection work. It also allows us to understand how we create anxiety and tension in multi-dog households.

I hope that you too can become 'obsessed' with functional characters after reading this book, and that you can help someone else to become equally so. Only by a growing obsession can we upgrade the lives of all dogs. Understanding them at a deeper level and truly getting to grips with all their communications will improve their lives immeasurably.

Thank you so much for taking the time to read my book. Written during three national 'lockdowns' in England, it is for the love of dogs everywhere.

Today's Dogs & Beyond

Rushing from place to place, appointment to appointment, work, children, shopping – we are often overly busy these days. All the commotion of our busy schedule can create quite a lot of stress for some dogs and excessive amounts for others. Exercise is often a race around the block or a quick run in the park. Diets are over-processed and not as healthy as they should be, which is also the case for humans. Anxiety, stress, unhealthy food and, often, a mentally understimulated lifestyle, all have a bearing on a dog's behaviour. Dogs will always outwardly show the pressures they are under within.

Over the past 30 years, I have seen a steady increase in dogs with behaviour problems. The most worrying part of this is that these are serious aggression issues, not just jumping up at visitors or pulling on the lead. However, in terms of knowledge and skills to help resolve behaviour problems, there is no denying that we have come a long way even in just the past 20 years. But we must do more. We need to understand our pets at a much deeper level. In her online course 'Complete Canine Wellness', Dr Isla Fishburn states that 'dogs are genetically ancient canines that live in a modern-day world'. She also tells us that 'they are living, emotional, sensory and cellular beings – they are an ecosystem'. How many of us see our dogs in this way? How many stop to consider what is going on *inside* our pets – what they are thinking, sensing, feeling, experiencing? We must become more acquainted with the many layers that our dogs consist of, and not just walking, feeding and cuddling.

If we enhanced our canine communication skills, I believe that we could improve dogs' lives still further. Yes, we have done a great job even in just the last ten years, but there is much more to do. We need to do our best to prevent the behaviour problems that lead many of them to a rescue centre, or Rainbow Bridge. Dogs should not end up at either of these destinations because nobody took the trouble to understand their 'language' and individual characteristics.

In the past, breed rescue charities have asked me to assess dogs in their own homes, before they are rehomed through no fault of their own. On one occasion, the dog under assessment was nearly nine years old and was being rehomed because it had bitten the owner's granddaughter. The owner told me that, ever since it was a puppy, the grandchildren had been encouraged to make a fuss of the dog while it was in its bed. They also told me the dog had raised its lip occasionally to the children during these fussing sessions. However, they had chastised the dog for doing so, and it had seemed fine after that. On the day of the bite incident, the youngest grandchild had rushed up to the dog to hug it. Internally I shuddered, and thought how patient that dog had been for all those years. I really wanted to share with these people why dogs do not understand hugging and kissing but reminded myself that I was not there to do a behaviour consultation and carried on with the form-filling.

The dog was subsequently rehomed to a family without children. I often think of that lovely dog and how he must have felt in his first few weeks and months in his new home. It breaks my heart to think of his emotional distress, being parted from his original 'family' purely because of miscommunication.

Numerous rescue centres are dealing with the aftermath of the lack of knowledge in canine communication. We need to change this. There needs to be a better understanding of dogs at a deeper level, and a more considered placement of puppies by those that bring them into the world. The more we understand canine communication and functional characters, the easier it would be for rescue centres to place dogs in new homes more accurately. Recently I have searched long and hard for a new dog. However, written underneath every little face that I could easily take home is the monotonous statement 'cannot live with other dogs'! I understand that rescue centres want to ensure dogs do not return to them, but are there really that many dogs that cannot get on with others, given the right circumstances and owner?

Could we ever get to a stage where there is just one rescue centre per country, or county, instead of hundreds? Maybe not. Maybe that is a somewhat optimistic view. However, suppose we strive to improve the lives of dogs everywhere, by understanding them as an individual, a functional character, and not just a breed or simply a species? In that case, we may well end up reducing the number of rescue centres along the way. Dogs give us so much. We owe it to them to increase our knowledge of them as an ecosystem, their internal requirements, communication subtleties *and* functional character.

By understanding dogs at a much deeper, cellular level, and their functional character, we can help create lives tailored to individuals, not just the species or the breed. Imagine if breeders could place each functional character into an appropriate home where the lifestyle complemented the individual puppy. Can you visualise all socialising and training sessions tailored to suit individual puppies and dogs? Understanding the importance of canine calming signals and the significance of a species-appropriate diet is vital in improving the lives of all dogs.

'The whole wellness of the dog is paramount to good life and behaviour.'

– Dr Isla Fishburn

Today, there is a vast difference in opinion about what constitutes 'health' for our beloved pets. Many dog owners follow their vet's advice on food and feeding without question. However, a growing number of enlightened owners seek to know more about making 'healthspan equal lifespan', as Dr Isla Fishburn so succinctly puts it.

Vets train hard for five or six years to learn everything they need to know medically to heal our pets for us when they fall ill. Long-standing veterinary professionals have shared with me that there is no tuition on canine diet and nutrition during this time, save what the large kibble manufacturers tell them. Also, only two hours of their six-year course is devoted to dog behaviour. So, unless they study these two important areas of canine care in their own time, their knowledge remains scant.

In the UK, it is no secret that most vet surgeries are owned by the top four veterinary corporations – CVS, Medivet, Pets at Home and Independent Vetcare. These corporate giants want as much buck for their bang as possible. So, once in practice, most vets are under real pressure to make a good revenue for the large corporations from the sale of their particular brand of food. A couple of long-standing vets have told me that they are offered significant incentives to sell dry food. Is it any wonder that vets have a vested interest in dogs eating kibble? I fear that dog owners have now become nothing more than cash cows in many UK areas. Countless chemicals, pills and reconstituted, unhealthy foods are available for the smallest of ailments, and it all gets washed down with as big a bill as possible. The number of 'special' diets on the market now, and the way they are endlessly prescribed, is a worry for the future. Sadly, it is not James Herriot anymore. Spreadsheet-focused, revenue-chasing conglomerates have replaced many of the traditional, friendly professionals who connect so well with their clients.

In my personal dealings with vets for my dogs, they never cease to alarm me with their uncompromising belief that kibble is the healthiest diet. The science behind the internal and digestive health of our pets seems to be of little interest to either kibble-peddling vets or the dry food manufacturers. So the relentless insistence of those 'qualified professionals' who are adamant that dry dog food is healthy for our beloved pets, and those that believe them, means an ever-increasing number of digestively compromised dogs. We are creating a world of nutritionally distressed dogs and, as Dr Isla Fishburn tells us in her online course, 'a nutritionally distressed bitch will give birth to nutritionally distressed puppies'. Pups fed on processed food may find it harder to transition to a fresh food diet, particularly if:

1   The litter is weaned onto dry, processed food by the breeder.

2   New owners continue feeding this dry diet during the first three months of life.

At a seminar in Bradford, UK, in early 2020, Dr Conor Brady related details of a study done by Zing-Yang Kuo in 1967. Three groups of Chow pups were fed different diets during their imprinting period. One group was fed soybeans, one on plant material, and the other on meat and bones. By the time these pups were three months old, only the group fed on meat and bones would consider eating novel foods. For the other Chow puppies, they would not eat anything else. Often, new owners who want to feed their puppy a healthy raw diet have problems doing so, and the Kuo study helps to explain why. At the time of writing, I have been unable to find similar but more up-to-date research.

It is a pity that so many professionals choose to ignore the science regarding feeding a fresh food, species-appropriate diet. However, it is significant that the international membership of the Raw Feeding Veterinary Society is growing. Hopefully, very soon, all raw feeders will have access to an enlightened veterinary practice that does not admonish them for choosing a species-specific diet over processed fodder.

During my research for pro-raw vets in the UK, I came across this admirable statement:

'We would like to change the current veterinary model and be incentivised by health, in other words, be paid to keep pets healthy.'

– WYLIE VET CENTRE IN BRENTWOOD, ESSEX

The Wylie statement, together with the fact that they sell the fresh food diet, suggests that this veterinary practice is guided by the science, not the salesmen of dry food manufacturers. I wish more of us had access to great pro-raw vets such as these:

➤ Wylie Vets (see www.wylievets.com/wylie-nourished and www.wylievets.com/news/species-appropriate-nutrition)

➤ Towerwood Vets (www.towerwoodvets.co.uk/services/nutrition/raw-feeding)

➤ https://holisticvet.co.uk

We all want our dogs to live longer because saying goodbye to them at a young age is hugely distressing. Let us look in a little more detail at these areas:

1   Health and wellbeing – how this can be compromised by diet.

2   Behaviour – why this is often misunderstood or misread.

3   Communication – why it is easy to miss vital cues.

4   Socialising – tailoring it to the individual.

5   Training – simplifying the process.

1. Health and wellbeing

Why don't we feed cows on meat, or give captive lions feline dry food? Because we provide them with the type of food that they are designed to eat – what their digestive systems have evolved over many hundreds, if not thousands of years, to absorb.

'A dog's wellness is compromised if not fed with species-specific food.'

– Dr Isla Fishburn

We all know that what we eat affects our health and wellbeing, and it is no different for our pets. Diet can drastically compromise health and wellbeing, which is why I have dedicated a whole chapter to the subject.

Also, how we feel and act from moment to moment can affect our dog's wellbeing. For example, an anxious owner who is continually tense and panicky will have a nervous dog. Our pets are so in tune with us that they pick up on our emotions and energy – good and not so good. Ever shouted at the television or punched the air in excitement and seen your dog dash into another room?

2. Behaviour

Behaviour is *anything* a dog does. When training your dog to sit, you teach them the 'behaviour' of putting their back end on the floor. In humans, the 'behaviour' of operating a car is called driving.

So how do we know what is and isn't acceptable behaviour? After all, two dogs growling and interacting roughly with their mouths wide open showing all their 'armoury' is undoubtedly aggression, yes? No! The subtle difference is the wide-open mouth, which translates to 'I'm just playing'. Because 80 per cent of dog play involves teeth, most interactions between dogs can look 'aggressive'. When talking about aggression these days, I prefer to use the term 'reactive' as it is less provocative. However, this is not necessarily helpful because all behaviours are 'actions', and all actions are 'reactive'. For example, your alarm goes off in the morning and you 'react' by getting out of bed or turning off the alarm. The dictionary describes 'reactive' as 'showing a response to a stimulus'. However, when the response becomes over-reactive, there may be a problem. Some reasons for over-reactivity are visible and logical, for example:

➤ A dog has stitches after an operation and snaps at other dogs that get too close.

➤ A dog with cropped ears and a docked tail gets a hard time from others because they cannot naturally signal their feelings or intentions.

However, there are instances when 'issues' are invisible, for example, dogs with cancer, or internal aches and pains. Suppose these individuals do not allow others from their social group to get as close to them as before? In that case, we may see aggression *before* we see the internal health issue manifested.

When medical reasons for a behaviour change are ruled out, other factors such as diet and lifestyle need to be examined. Also, recent changes to or losses in their social group need to be investigated. Loss in their social group can relate to a human as well as another dog. Grief can overwhelm some dogs, just like people. The Observer functional character is probably more susceptible to distress after a loss than any other.

The way we raise, care for, socialise and train our dogs has changed immeasurably over the past 50 years. A significant number of changes have been brilliant for dogs – the proliferation of canine enrichment by companies such as Kong and Nina Ottosson are great examples. The increase in veterinary professionals specialising in species-appropriate diets and less chemically contaminated lives for our pets has been very welcome. Much of the latter is down to the tireless work of Catherine O'Driscoll. Her tremendous input into the dog world via her charity, Canine Health Concern, and her books, has inspired many dog professionals. Sadly, Catherine passed away at the time of writing this chapter, and so the dog world has lost one of its fiercest advocates.

➤ www.canine-health-concern.org.uk

➤ www.catherineodriscoll.com

However, while all this is brilliant for the dog world, many dog owners still have a shortfall of understanding regarding calming signals. Appreciating these is a fundamental part of 21st century dog ownership if we want to live in more harmony with our pets. We have recently started to understand another significant aspect of our dogs – their functional character. Apart from identifying the purpose that an individual serves as a social group animal, the functional character also:

➤ explains the dynamics of group composition, and how we can create conflict and tension in a multi-dog household

➤ determines how they socialise, and their social interactions with other dogs and people

➤ explains why it may not be a good idea to breed from

certain individuals

➤ helps establish which individuals would be best suited for assistance dog or police dog roles, competition obedience, work with autistic children, etc.

➤ enables us to choose our next dog more efficiently to complement an existing social group, rather than causing any friction between individuals

➤ assists breeders in placing their puppies with potential new owners more accurately.

A greater understanding of all the above is vital if we want to:

➤ reduce the number of dogs in rescue centres

➤ reduce the number of rescue centres on the planet

➤ enjoy more positive 'meet and greets' with our dogs

➤ prevent 'breedist' insults and verbal abuse at dog parks

➤ increase the number of dogs that stay in their original homes

➤ stem the tide of dogs that develop serious behaviour problems

➤ pick puppies more astutely for the role we want them to perform.

Dogs are often labelled 'optimistic', 'selectively deaf', 'intolerant', 'impulsive', 'calm', 'giddy', and many others. These labels, although they may describe a dog's personality, or a particular action at any given moment, do not help us to understand why they are the way they are, or:

➤ how to increase the speed of their learning

➤ why they do not want to socialise with the dog next door

➤ how to avoid a tirade of barking when you try to relax at home

➤ why they are scared to venture out of the front door and go for a walk.

Getting a dog to venture outside can be a difficult task if you have an Observer functional character. Mostly, even coaxing with food or toys may not get this individual remotely interested in going over the threshold. These quivering, fearful dogs often end up visiting the vet or a behaviourist. Or we plug in a pheromone diffuser, hoping for change. However, if we understood the quirks of their functional character, we could solve their confidence issue with a better option.

An Overseer functional character could look 'aggressive' most of the time because of its pre-programmed 'quality control' duties. And the muzzle 'punch' from a Peacekeeper is an action that could easily be misread by two inexperienced owners. If a Defender steps in to perform some peacekeeping, then the muzzle punch may look much more high octane. Imagine how that would go down between two first-time dog owners at the dog park if the Defender in question is a Rottie or a Staffie! (We will explore the different characters in the next chapter.)

Here is another example of what could be misconstrued as 'aggression'. At a recent 'Beyond the Breed' functional character workshop, we had two Defenders meeting and greeting – an intact male Spaniel and a spayed female crossbreed. As the female approached the male, he snapped at her, which his owner said was unusual for him. A slight injury from the day before the event made the male unwilling to display weakness in the presence of another Defender. He snapped at her to get her to move away from him.

Our dogs offer endless behaviours, and there are an infinite number of potential behaviour problems that can occur with them. When working with clients, I help them to appreciate the basic needs of their dog. We explore potential issues and then discuss how they can be resolved. Some of our basic requirements for a dog are listed below.

Healthy skin

Healthy skin starts with a species-appropriate diet of fresh food. Skin problems, such as itchy or dry patches, are uncomfortable for dogs and humans alike. If a dog feels sore or in pain with a skin condition, their energy level changes, which then impacts their emotions and, consequently, how they interact with their environment and those around them.

Sense of peace

For dogs, a sense of peace culminates from good food and exercise; a calm environment; feeling part of a social group; reliable and confident leadership; and company and affection. A dog is an energy system, just like a human. At a cellular level, a dog is always assessing 'Am I safe?' There is less potential for safety when walking along a busy street with their owner because the energy in this environment is not calm. Living or exercising in this type of environment may certainly cause an Observer more anxiety, creating additional fear in an already naturally fearful individual. Dogs living in fear much of the time are more likely to have ear problems or noise phobia. Let me explain.

Ever since ancient Greek medicine, over 2,000 years ago, it has been thought that different emotions are stored in, and affect, different areas of the body. Traditional Chinese medicine (TCM), including tai chi, qigong and acupuncture, also teaches us that various organs of the body are affected by different emotions, and that various emotions can cause illness or disease to certain organs. In my qigong classes, we are shown exercises to help unblock or remove stagnant energy (*qi* or *chi* – life force) from the body using both physical movement and verbal sound.

Emotions are always flowing throughout the body but if we, or our dogs, live with a certain emotion for a prolonged period, it can accumulate in one particular organ. For example, anger accumulates in the liver and can cause digestive issues; excessive stress can affect the adrenal glands; and fear, fright and shock can cause problems for the kidneys. In TCM, we learn that the kidneys play a big part in our lives as they send *qi* to other organs in the body if they are low in energy. We are apparently born with a certain amount of *qi*, which depletes as we age. Quantum physics teaches us that everything is energy, and it is widely accepted that we are energy beings, and are all vibrating at every moment. Research has shown that emotions vibrate at various frequencies – see www.cosmicminds.net/how-an-emotional-vibrational-frequency-chart-can-help-you. The kidneys are said to resonate with the vibration of fear, which vibrates at around 100 hertz. If we, or our dogs, experience fear or insecurity for a prolonged period, this can cause the feeling of fear to become chronic.

Life force energy or chi/qi is my 'tool' as a reiki master to help reactive dogs, which can be done in person or from a distance, and those of you who work with energy will understand this. This life force flows around our bodies, and our dogs, by way of energy pathways, or meridians. All internal organs are set on certain meridians and are therefore connected to various parts of the outside of the body. The kidneys are linked to the bladder and the ears. Everyone, at one time or another, has witnessed a dog, or most likely a puppy, wetting themselves uncontrollably. This usually happens when a dog is in a situation that it sees as unsafe, but more particularly if they suffer an extreme fright. The reason for this is that a fright can cause a sudden loss of *qi* from the kidneys, which causes the bladder to empty involuntarily.

➤ www.greekmedicine.net/hygiene/Emotions_and_Organs.html

➤ www.emotionsandbody.com/2016/11/kidneys-emotional-conflicts-that-can_10.html

If the negative emotion of fear is ignored and builds up in the kidneys, it can also affect ears and may cause problems such as noise phobia. Because the *qi* in kidneys depletes as we and our dogs age, and because these important organs are connected to the ears, it explains why hearing is affected in elderly individuals of both species.

Traditional Chinese medicine includes the five elements theory – water, fire, earth, metal and wood, which are used to explain the functioning of the body. The kidneys are linked to the element of water – see the excellent diagram for all the elements and the organs connected to them at www.tcmworld.org/wp-content/uploads/2015/02/the-five-elements.jpg. So, with this, and the research of Dr Masaru Emoto in mind (see www.shiftfrequency.com/dr-masaru-emotos-scientific-experiments), try these tips recommended by Dr Isla Fishburn:

➤ Use only filtered water for your dogs.

➤ Put the water in a glass or stone dish rather than metal.

➤ Place the dish on a mat where words such as love, gratitude, wealth and joy are written.

To help dogs further with their sense of peace, we should give them exercise that is not rushed. Racing around the block or park because we are hastily trying to get to work or an appointment does not provide dogs with calm or a sense of peace. Likewise, having to jog with their owner for an entire dog walk, without a chance to sniff or properly empty their bowels or bladder, is neither mentally stimulating nor enjoyable. Planning more time for our walks to enable us to stop at certain places to soak up the atmosphere with our pets is not often easy in our busy lives. I understand that. However, rather than striding out on a kind of route march, we need to take time for our dogs, and ourselves – giving both species a sense of peace. Stopping from time to time to just let our pets sniff, and for us to take in the scenery, is so relaxing and great for our stress levels!

We can also provide a great learning experience and a sense of peace when walking outdoors with new puppies and young dogs by slowing down and stopping from time to time. Young individuals need to learn in their own time, so stopping and waiting for them to explore is essential. They need to satisfy their curiosity about everything in the big wide world as this is how they acquire knowledge and deposit experience into their memory banks. After investigation, even from afar, the learning experience is stored in the individual's mind for future reference. A dog's biography (its history) becomes its biology (its ecosystem). So, everything must be considered, both when nurturing a young individual and when trying to determine their functional character.

Restful sleep

Having somewhere comfortable, safe, and quiet to curl up is essential because dogs sleep between 14 and 18 hours each day. An indoor 'den' (dog cage/crate) covered on all sides except the doorway, and filled with plenty of bedding that can be made into a nest, is ideal. Choose a quiet place in your home to position your pet's sleeping area – somewhere away from the hustle and bustle of the family where they will feel safe and able to curl up to sleep. Dr Isla Fishburn calls these quiet places 'den sites' as they mimic the places that wolf cubs go to feel safe.

Dogs should be left alone when in their safe sleeping place. At mealtimes, or if the family want to spend time with their pet, the dog should be called to them, rather than anyone approaching the sleeping area, as it gives them a choice. Some functional characters are not inclined to be physically close to anyone or have their own personal space bubble 'invaded'.

Ability to think clearly

A dog's ability to think clearly can be hampered by things such as a hectic home life, digestive problems caused by an inadequate diet, feeling too hot or too cold, or feeling hungry or unsafe.

Feeling safe is vital for dogs, and it is a *feeling* rather than *thinking*. Unconsciously, they are constantly scanning their environment for 'safety'. If a dog meets something or someone that it *feels* is safe, it will move towards the thing or person, and if it feels unsafe, it will move away. The moving towards or away is known as the orienting response, and it explains how an individual responds towards something new in its environment. Dogs must learn at their own speed, and certain functional characters will naturally orient away from more things/people than others – Observers, for example, who are life's 'worrywarts'! Dogs should never be forced, or pulled, towards something or someone new because their only choice apart from the orienting response is the stress response.

During the stress response, dogs are unable to think clearly, and may become highly reactive. Further socialising may then be hampered because the stress response would override the orienting response, particularly if the situation involved the same people/things or environment(s). For example, an Observer puppy is taken to a local 'puppy party' run by inexperienced people who do not supervise the puppies' interactions. The Observer puppy would find the whole event terrifying and may spend the entire 'party' in a stress response. Some owners at these types of events are encouraged to compel their pups to meet other puppies. I have had many appointments with owners who are at their wits' end due to this 'encouragement'. Many of them now had an adult dog that screamed like a banshee every time another dog glanced their way.

We must understand more about how dogs communicate, and quickly, as this will enable us to make meeting and greeting, at least, better experiences for them. The more knowledge we have regarding functional characters and calming signals, the more we can help our pets. With your help, we can start spreading the word and 'infect' the world with our enthusiasm to understand dogs at their deepest level. Let us use our knowledge of functional characters to try and get the changes that many agree would be great to see:

➤ *The need for fewer dog rescue centres.* Imagine if breeders were able to place the right functional character in the right home? Would this not mean fewer dogs being given up as older pups or adolescents due to the family's inability to cope? I do not think we could banish the need for rescue centres altogether because there will always be those who buy a puppy without the necessary research and preparation. During the first two years of ownership, there are many factors to dog ownership, and adolescence is a particularly trying time! Many people are also not prepared for the house training, socialising, basic manners training, etc. How many puppy owners are willing to pause on a walk for their puppy to take in everything? There is so much more to raising a well-balanced, healthy canine than just teaching them to sit, shake a paw and walk on a lead. A dog does not become the ultimate scholar because it can leave a full food bowl for ages until instructed to eat, and not chase livestock.

➤ *Fewer over-reactive dogs at behavioural consultations.* Yes, as a behaviourist, I would very much like to see fewer stressed-out or over-reactive dogs.

➤ *More knowledgeable, empowered pet owners.* It is excellent to know that many dog owners already understand why the correct diet is so essential. Similarly, an increasing number of owners also understand how energy levels affect behaviour and how to socialise and train their pet according to its functional character. I know that many of these owners are spreading the word, so let's keep growing in knowledge and numbers!

➤ *More dogs staying with their first owner.* Knowledge is power, and owners with a great understanding of functional characters and calming signals can give their pet the best life possible.

3. Communication

It is easy to miss vital clues in canine communication because dogs identify through scent, which is a crucial part of chemical communication between individuals. Their visual communication is very subtle. For example, an ear flick, a lip lick and tail carriage height are easily missed. By studying numerous dogs and their interactions and body language, it is possible to become skilful at recognising what is going on between individuals.

Most people know the 'play bow', which is canine shorthand for 'everything I do after this is playing!' But what about teeth out during play? I would guess that many people think this is a precursor to an attack. Dog games are rough, and 80 per cent involve teeth. During play, a wide-open mouth means 'although I'm showing my armoury, I am using it for playing'. Necks are made for games too, but many owners are horrified when their dog bites or hangs off another dog's neck or pins them down by the neck. Another misconception is when a dog lays on its back and exposes its belly – most people think their pet wants a belly rub or tummy tickle. However, the real meaning is quite different.

Calming signals are easy to miss, as they are more subtle than some body language. Lip-licking and yawning are so often interpreted as hunger and tiredness. The main reason for this is because we feel the need to understand everything in human terms, rather than looking at these signals from the canine's point of view.

One of the best books around for understanding calming signals and canine communication is *On Talking Terms with Dogs: Calming Signals* by Turid Rugaas, a Norwegian dog trainer. I think everyone should read this before getting a dog, and every child should read *The Canine Commandments* by Dr Kendal Shepherd, and take part in the games of the Blue Dog Programme (www. pawsability.co.uk/dogtrainingnotes/dogsandchildren.htm).

Because dogs communicate and identify through scent, their communication can be challenging to understand. For example, an owner might assume that their dog is 'selectively deaf' because they will not come back to them when they call. However, when a dog is fully focused on a smell they are unable to concentrate on anything else. They are not multi-taskers! Suppose they have their nose down a rabbit hole; their brain is effectively 'out to lunch', and so calling them doesn't usually work until they have finished sniffing.

4. Socialising

I can remember a television programme in the 1980s called *Dogs with Dunbar* in which groups of puppies were off the lead together. Everything was fun for the puppies as they were taught to come, sit and settle, all while being distracted by the others in the group. Sometimes there was a bit of mayhem, but overall it was a great learning experience for the youngsters. It was super to see so many puppies having fun together while learning some basic training. Thirty years ago, this type of puppy socialising was groundbreaking. Dr Dunbar's innovative puppy programme may well have been the forerunner to what we know today as 'puppy parties'. Unfortunately, many of the 'parties' these days lack appropriate interaction management and some degree of basic training – they are a recipe for behaviour problems further down the line. On the other side of the coin, some events do not permit any freedom of expression. It is a fine line between allowing too much liberty and not enough. Puppies need to develop their social skills while also having the freedom to express who they are as individuals, but not at the expense of potential trauma to another puppy. However, constant interruption of communication between individuals can cause frustration for one or both parties and create problems later on.

It is undisputed that puppies need to be exposed – desensitised – to a wide variety of people, other dogs and animals, noises, places, etc. Everyone knows that social interactions help to support wellness and early learning. However, too much freedom of expression can overload their energy system, and their nervous system. Physical exercise increases adrenaline, and therefore the energy system of an individual. Increased adrenaline in one dog can cause an overreaction from an unexercised individual – one on the lead or one mooching around minding their own business. Every day, on dog walks up and down the land, dogs are allowed to rush up to others. An adrenaline-fuelled dog with a lack of meet-and-greet skills is, unfortunately, often asking for trouble. Sadly, on these occasions, it is down to the owner whose dog is under control to make excuses about why their pet snapped.

Our hectic lives contribute to a perpetual sensory overload for our pets. When the nervous system is overloaded, it can create stress and lead it to become erratic. For the owners of Observers and Overseers, in particular, this is not great. It is also bad news in the long term because an unstable nervous system can lead to irrational behaviours and rage. However, this is different to 'rage syndrome', which has been unfairly linked to Cocker Spaniels. Many other breeds have suffered from this disorder, which is also called idiopathic aggression because it has no known cause. Dr Ilana Reisner DVM has done the most research into this subject, and she concludes that it is a condition that follows family lines. It is associated with low levels of serotonin. Serotonin is known as the 'happy chemical' and is one of the brain chemicals (neurotransmitters) with a calming effect (see https://mental-health-matters.com/the-chemical-imbalance-in-mental-health-problems). Similar findings regarding low serotonin levels were also found in violent mental patients and prison inmates.

Low serotonin seems such a small thing, but it can dramatically affect an individual. Understanding this does help drive home just how easy it is for our pets to become out of kilter emotionally and mentally. Because a dog is constantly and instinctively scanning the environment for 'safety', its emotional state can change according to how safe it feels in any given moment. Walking our dogs in nature helps to calm the nervous system, as does allowing them to rest for their required daily amount of 14–18 hours, somewhere den-like and away from busy parts of the home. Rebalancing the nervous system can be extremely difficult, especially if there is trauma attached. Functional character and other factors will also play their part. Supportive therapies such as sound therapy or other vibrational medicine modalities can help, on top of supporting the dog's physical needs. Alternatively, you may find that your pet calms after sniffing or licking rose or frankincense water, as these help reduce adrenaline levels from a state of over-arousal or trauma. However, when it comes to what a dog needs to help rebalance its nervous system, it can be like asking 'How long is a piece of string?' because it will vary from individual to individual.

Many dogs struggle with the naturally fizzy nature and energy of Spaniels, Staffies and Border Collies. The Defender and Overseer functional characters can also be very exuberant. Imagine, then, the energy level of a Staffie who is also a Defender at a large gathering of puppies. Suppose this event is run by people who are not experienced in dog behaviour, body language or calming signals. Some puppies could go home very distressed, or high on adrenaline. In the past, I have had clients who have returned from a 'socialising' event with a very traumatised young pet. Those in charge need to fully understand canine communication and how puppies should meet and greet appropriately. However, it is essential not to control and intervene before a puppy 'conversation' has even started. Knowledge of functional characters is infinitely useful in these situations.

Past clients who were the owners of a pup labelled a 'troublemaker' have been visibly upset while recounting the episode at a puppy party to me. Some of these owners stopped socialising their pet altogether, choosing to walk them exceedingly early in the morning and late at night when nobody else was around. The problem then is that they ended up with a seriously under-socialised and under-desensitised adult dog. Teaching an adult dog how to meet and greet appropriately is not as easy as with a puppy. Helping these owners see that their dog was not a misfit, and why they were a bit of a head-banger as a youngster, was extremely rewarding. They gained more confidence about future socialising and meeting and greeting. Many of these clients told me that their dog was very calm at home, but I explained that this is connected to energy. A dog that lives in a quieter environment or social group will elicit a more relaxed response because their energy system is calmer.

For the Observer functional character, a puppy party may not be a great place. If the group is allowed to become rowdy, there is less potential for the Observer's safety. To aid their safety, they would probably seek refuge under a chair, or their owner's legs. Imagine their distress if they were then pulled out and forced into the path or energy of the other pups to play. During 30 years of running puppy classes, I have seen many owners pulling their pet out from underneath a chair and saying 'go and play'. Trauma of any kind is much harder for a puppy to overcome than an adult dog. The distress becomes etched into the individual at a cellular level, and so their biography then becomes their biology. A puppy enduring this type of ordeal would probably go on to have a lifetime aversion to other dogs. Many people will have witnessed a dog screaming with fear because another dog has simply looked at them. Unfortunately, because fear is learned at a deep, cellular level, due to it being connected with the individual's very survival, dogs cannot 'unlearn' it. Once the trauma has been thrust deep into a dog, there is little chance of a full recovery. Suppose a puppy has suffered abuse at the hands of a person with a beard: in that case, beards will always elicit an instant, and seemingly irrational, meltdown.

Socialising and desensitising are never really finished. It is not 'job done' after taking a puppy to a few 'parties', a couple of sessions at daycare, or a six-week puppy course. It is for life. The socialisation 'window' closes around the age of three months. After that, it is no longer socialising, but desensitising, and this should be done throughout the dog's life. Every new thing/person/situation they experience is desensitising them for the next and helping them to become more 'socialised'. It is vital to desensitise a dog to everything, everywhere, all the time, to enable them to cope with whatever may happen in their life. Everything they see, hear, touch, taste and smell, wherever they go and at any time, are all stored as memories. The experiences and memories help develop the individual. Socialising puppies should be done with older dogs who have been well socialised and who are social individuals, for example, Peace-keepers, Follower or Nanny functional characters. Overseers and Defenders are generally too gregarious for meeting and greeting with puppies, and Guides are too aloof. Socialising adult dogs should be appropriate for the functional character of the individual being socialised and for the dogs they are meeting.

5. Training

We all nurture and care for our pets, just as we do our children. And, like your dogs, mine are part of the family. There has been an increase in dogs being treated like babies in recent years, but whatever their size, shape, type or cuteness, they still have a canine brain. They are not baby humans, furry or otherwise! However, like all human toddlers, dogs need boundaries, guidelines and rules. It is also an excellent idea to teach our pets some crucial life skills, such as a reliable recall and walking nicely on the lead when we are out. Personal space exercises, such as relaxing and settling on a mat when visitors come, are also essential for a great life together.

Dogs need to learn in their own time, and training sessions should be short and fun. We should also structure the training according to the learning ability of the individual's functional character if we want to avoid getting frustrated. Frustration produces an alteration in our biochemistry, which is picked up by our pets. Different functional characters learn at different speeds and in different ways, and they have different outlooks and expectations. A 15-minute training session for a Guide may not pose much of a problem mentally, as they would be seeking ways to elevate the learning. However, most Followers and Observers would probably have information overload by about the second minute!

Puppy training should be slowed down during a fear period, with nothing in the way of changes or challenges to either their training or life. Play is awesome for puppies and dogs alike, and it is educational. The 'Jazz Up, Settle Down' exercise that Dr Ian Dunbar teaches is excellent for all dogs, particularly puppies. As we have discussed, an excess of 'happy' creates the same over-arousal as too much stress. For this reason, teaching a puppy to sit still for a short time while playing with family members or other puppies is, I believe, highly beneficial.

Striving to see things from a dog's perspective will help us to understand them more. Perhaps then we will see fewer communication breakdowns between the species, human and canine. Functional characters are a big part, but they are not the whole answer. There will always be situations and circumstances where two dogs don't ever see eye to eye, and you may never work out why that is. Even though the functional characters seem compatible, it may be more to do with the myriad of other characteristics of the individuals concerned. Although dogs are a social species, it does not mean they are social to every other individual – just like us!

Let's see if we can infect the world with our enthusiasm to:

➤ know dogs at a deeper level

➤ get acquainted with a dog's ecosystem

➤ nurture them mentally as well as physically

➤ care for them emotionally as well as spiritually

➤ and understand their functional characters and foibles!

Functional Characters Explained

Functional characters consist of Guides and Followers. Anything other than a Guide is classed as a Follower. Followers can be further broken down into certain functional characters – see table below.

GUIDES	FOLLOWERS
Guide	Defender
	Overseer
	Observer
	Hunter
	Follower
	Peacekeeper
	Lone Individual

An individual's functional character explains the functional purpose of that individual within a social group. There would be two Guides (leaders, or alphas) in an undomesticated group – one male and one female. Guides are the group's decision-makers – they decide where to hunt, what to pursue and how long to stay there. Therefore the group cannot survive without their decision-making abilities. Guides are the only individuals that breed within a social group and are often referred to as 'the breeding pair'. The remainder of the group would consist of an assortment of Follower characters – Defenders, Hunters, Peacekeepers, etc., but by no means would there be an equal number of each. Indeed, social groups can exist without some of the characters, although not without at least one Guide.

Briefly, very generally, and not in any particular order, functional characters are:

GUIDE	A self-preserving, 'go-to' individual, a good problem-solver
LONE INDIVIDUAL	Has a small personal space bubble, similar to the Guide
DEFENDER	Chunkiest in a litter and a good problem-solver
OBSERVER	Alerts group to potential danger, a real worrywart!
OVERSEER	The group's eccentric!
PEACEKEEPER	A very appeasing individual
FOLLOWER	The 'standby crew'!
HUNTER	A fast, agile individual, hard to keep weight on
NANNY/GUARDIAN	An 'associate character' of any of the above that adopts caregiving and teaching duties to young pups

Functional characters explain the social interactions and dynamics of any group of canines – change the group, or an individual, and you change the dynamics. In other words, it explains why Rover gets on with Fido and Freddie but is an entirely different dog if Yogi is around. Also, functional character determines how individuals interact with each other and within their environment at any given moment. The functional character of an individual is set before birth, possibly at conception, and is not defined by breed or breed mix. Other canines easily recognise all functional characters, and all characters will generally defer to a Guide.

Functional *characteristics* were first observed by the renowned wolf biologist Dr Gordon Haber, in the 40+ years that he studied wild wolves in Alaska. From his findings, it is clear the same characteristics can be observed in dogs, whose DNA is 98.8% wolf and are descended from the same wolf ancestor as the Grey Wolf. For those who would like to read more about Dr Haber's detailed and intimate studies of the Alaskan wolves, I can highly recommend his book *Among Wolves.* Marybeth Holleman used Dr Haber's extensive notes and photographs to write the book after his untimely death in 2009 when his light aeroplane crashed.

Dr Isla Fishburn has also made detailed studies of functional characters, both with dogs and with wolves. Her wealth of knowledge in this area can now be accessed by everyone online at https://kachinacanine.com/complete-wellness. As dog owners and guardians, Dr Isla's work enables us to benefit from knowing our dogs in more depth. From this knowledge, we can then give them the best life possible during their short time with us.

Functional characters explain why, for example:

➤ not all Border Collies make the grade as farm dogs

➤ some individuals training to be guide dogs get rehomed before they complete their course

➤ police dogs are often put up for adoption part way through their rigorous training programme.

As an example, think about a Guide – a self-preserving individual that will not put itself in harm's way. What if that Guide is a police dog?

To illustrate my point about farm dogs, I will relate something that happened at one of our 2020 Beyond the Breed functional character workshops. A lovely attendee had brought her three Border Collies for assessment. She said that when they were working on her farm, one of them was quite happy to help with the sheep in the field but would not get involved in penning them inside her barn. It became clear at the workshop that the reluctant individual was a Guide. This Border Collie's unwillingness to get involved with working the sheep at close quarters clearly illustrates the Guide's self-preserving nature.

Although dogs have a true functional character based on their functional purpose as a social group animal, different environments, situations and group structures can influence the actions of an individual to show another character. For example – a Guide, Defender or Follower could take on a Peacekeeper role if the group it is with lacks this character. I have witnessed this several times at my daycare facility on the days when any of our Peacekeepers are not with us.

We have also seen Followers 'test', which makes them resemble an Overseer. It is possible, however, for any functional character to 'test'. 'Testing' is the Overseer's way of requesting calm and, once they have a less energetic environment, they become more relaxed. With individuals morphing into different characters, it often makes the task of identifying an individual's precise functional character somewhat complicated!

Apart from the environment, situation and other individuals, there are several other things to bear in mind when considering the functional character of an individual, such as:

a) *The predispositions of the breed, or breed mix of the individual* – for example, a Staffie may look like a Defender because, for the most part, this breed is naturally extrovert. Many German Shepherds could be mistaken for Observers because of their characteristic lunging behaviour. And farm-bred Border Collies from a working line may often resemble Overseers due to their intense stare and herding behaviour towards other individuals, which resembles 'testing'.

b) *Diet and digestion* – what a dog is 'fuelled' on makes a huge difference, not only to the individual's behaviour, but also their health. Feeding dry, over-processed biscuit-type food to a dog is similar to a human eating nothing but fast food at every meal. Sooner or later, digestive system problems will appear. A dog with internal health problems may manifest as a tetchy personality and therefore make a different functional character seem more likely than the individual's actual character.

During the 30+ years that I ran training classes, I frequently saw dogs coming into a new group who appeared to be Overseers because of their 'testing' and hyperactive behaviour. I often asked owners if they fed a particular brand of pet food, to which they replied, 'Yes, how did you know?' Hyperactivity is a common problem among dogs these days, and many dogs can look like Overseers when they are not. I believe the cause of most hyperactivity is due to the carb-rich food and 'treats' that many dogs are given. This is not a problem in and of itself, but it does make a great deal of difference when considering a tailored approach to care, socialising and training.

It is often easier to assess the functional characters of raw-fed individuals because processed food can affect a dog's behaviour and mask their functional character. Emotions, fuelled by their senses, are the driving force behind all dog behaviour, and emotions are impacted by diet. Hence feeding a species-specific fresh food diet is essential. In humans, it is our thoughts that fuel our emotions and, ultimately, our actions – 'as a person thinketh, so shall they be'. However, for both species, underneath all of this is energy. We are all energy beings, and everything is energy. This has been proven by Nobel prize-winning Danish physicist Niels Bohr. Each of us has a unique energy 'signature'. This field of energy radiates out from our body and can be measured scientifically – see www.reiki.org/articles/science-measures-human-energy-field.

c) *Health* – injury or illness may also affect the way an individual behaves towards others in a group. We discovered in Chapter 1 how this applies to a Defender functional character in particular.

d) *Safety* – dogs that can think clearly and feel safe in the moment can behave naturally – therefore their functional character is more easily seen and identified. Regardless of functional character, if an individual feels unsafe, they will respond in, or to, a situation in a way that makes a different character look more likely. Safety and clear thinking can be hampered by things such as feeling too hot or cold, feeling hungry, having digestive problems, or the environment being too busy or noisy.

e) *Immunology* – has the individual recently had a vaccination or been given an oral pesticide such as Fluralaner? Both can cause unseen and untold health issues internally for a dog and can drastically affect their behaviour as well as their long-term health.

Any of the above may distort one's perception of an individual's functional character. Discovering our dog's functional character is, therefore, a little more involved than just watching how they interact with, and within, a group of dogs.

Once we have determined our dog's functional character, we can begin to understand why they act and react the way they do in certain situations and around certain individuals. It also helps us to understand why there may be issues between specific individuals in a multi-dog household and, potentially, how to resolve them. However, any functional character can be pushed out of a group if it is superfluous to its requirements. A group knows what functional characters it needs to complement one another and survive, which is important to remember if you run a big group together as a dog professional, or are the proud owner of numerous dogs.

Because some functional characters are more susceptible to emotional distress than others, group dynamics and the emotional state of an individual will also affect its functional character *and* its interactions with other individuals in its social group. All of this brings us back to safety. When an individual feels safe, they are less likely to clash with others in their social group. They are also able to exhibit normal and natural behaviour according to their functional character.

Stress and fear are different for individual functional characters. What is highly stressful for an Observer or a Guide may only be mildly stressful for a Follower, and not scary in the slightest for a Defender. After an emotionally distressing event, the reactions of other group members (humans and dogs) will also have a bearing on how the individual character deals with the event.

Any individual can be afraid, but a well-socialised Guide may show less fear than an under-socialised Follower. Followers seem to have the broadest spectrum of difference – they range from finely built, timid individuals to more emotionally robust characters that resemble Defenders. Indeed, they can be some of the largest pups in a litter, but never have the chunky physique of the Defender.

'A Guide is strength through knowledge and a Defender is strength through confidence.'

– Dr Isla Fishburn

 **Guide**

Guides, sometimes referred to as Decision Makers, are the group leaders – what some may call the 'alpha'. They are priority individuals who decide what to do, where to go and how long to stay there – they are the 'go-to' individual for the whole group. For example, suppose a group were hunting and some were killed or lost, the remainder would go to the Guide to see what to do next. Without a Guide, social groups are unable to survive because no other individual has their decision-making ability.

As individuals, Guides are self-preserving and aloof. Their survival is more important than that of any other group member because no other functional character has their leadership expertise. Snobbish and socially isolated, Guides have a small social network of individuals to whom they feel strongly connected. Their independent nature means that they do not require as much contact with others in the group. They will, however, 'connect' to other individuals when they wish to teach, guide, lead and instruct. In a large social group, there would be two Guides – one male and one female. The female is ultimately the 'top dog' as she is, for the most part, the mother of most of the group, and therefore what binds the group together.

Although Guides are visually more striking, or can be the most stunningly marked puppy, they are often the last one left in a litter to sell. The main reason for being left behind is, I think, because they do not come forward to greet potential new owners. We would describe them as 'shy', and most people like to take home a pup that is not. People have often happily told me 'oh, my dog picked me'! The functional characters least likely to be at the front of the playpen when you visit a litter of puppies are mostly going to be the Guide, Lone Individual and Observer.

Having excellent maternal instinct makes female Guides great mothers and, as already discussed, these would be the only breeding individuals in a group. In an undomesticated social group, female Guides would suppress the seasons of other females in the group to prevent them breeding, although this would not always be effective. As young mums, Guides mostly do not produce a female Guide, as there are many more years of decision-making (guiding) ahead of them. Older females may give birth to one or two Guides, although not in every litter. In cases where there are two, there would be one of each sex.

Any female has a significant influence on what functional characters she produces, depending on her environment and social needs. An example of the impact of social needs in humans is the tendency for women to give birth to more boys than girls after a war. This phenomenon has become known as 'the returning soldier effect', explained by Professor Sir David Spiegelhalter in this article:

www.science20.com/david_spiegelhalter/why_are_more_boys_born_at_the_end_of_wars-154948

The Guide functional character can be quite challenging for a lot of people, particularly first-time dog owners, for several reasons:

➤ Guides are easily distracted if they become bored as their learning capability is huge. Once they have learnt something, they want to move on quickly. (In a training situation, a Guide frustrated with slow-paced learning could easily resemble an Overseer, minus the nipping!)

➤ They require much more mental stimulation than other characters because they have a low threshold for boredom. (Imagine a Border Collie Guide from a strong working line, living in an urban domestic environment with young children in the family, and no outlet for their cleverness. I have seen Border Collies in this sort of situation many times, and believe it is the main reason so many end up in rescue centres every year.)

➤ Due to their self-preserving nature, which is hard-wired, they may seem to be very stubborn. They weigh-up each situation for personal safety. For example, Dr Isla Fishburn was speaking at an event for police dog handlers, and a couple of officers were discussing one of the dogs. The dog in question was trained to perfection for what is known in this field as 'manwork' and for tracking criminals, and brilliant in a training environment. However, the dog would refuse to 'engage' on arrival at a live incident – it would just jump back into the officer's van. This dog was most definitely a Guide functional character!

➤ Guides are not keen on repetition for repetition's sake and like to do things *their* way. Doing things *their* way is probably the reason they are labelled 'stubborn'! I have a female Guide who, after a few repetitions, will move straight on to the end part, or her version of the finished exercise! This jumping ahead is another reason why Guides can be challenging for first-time owners. Those who are new to dog training often will not know exactly what the end of the exercise looks like or indeed should be.

Guides can make great assistance dogs due to their excellent problem-solving abilities and enormous propensity to learn. However, due to their self-preserving nature, they would not entertain a situation that could affect their safety. Overleaf are some examples of both problem-solving and self-preservation from my Guide, KD.

Problem-solving

Recently I discovered a lost bracelet under a bed but could not reach it. I called my Guide, who came and lay down next to where I was kneeling. I pointed towards the bracelet and asked her to 'get it' – her verbal cue for a retrieve. Although she has never been taught to crawl underneath furniture, she immediately started crawling towards the bracelet, picked it up, then turned around and crawled back out. Afterwards, I wished I had videoed it!

One evening at a training class, KD returned a dropped wallet to its owner. Nobody had seen the wallet drop to the floor except her, and she promptly trotted over, picked it up, and presented it to the gentleman who owned it. Another reason that makes this such a brilliant piece of problem-solving is that I have never taught her to take something to someone, only to return things to me.

Self-preservation

KD has always cleared away all the dog dishes after meals – I wait at the dishwasher, and she brings them to me one at a time. During the UK's first lockdown in the warm and sunny spring of 2020, I fed my dogs in the shade outside on the patio. To prevent flies from entering through the open patio doors, I had fastened a fly screen. It was one of those screens with magnets down the middle to provide easy access for pets. When I gave my Guide the cue to tidy the dishes, she raced out into the garden. I waited in the kitchen for her to return with the first dish. And waited. Then I went to see what had waylaid her. I laughed as I saw her standing outside with a dog dish in her mouth, wagging her tail like mad. Then I apologised to her for not considering that she would find it way too scary to come through the fly screen with a dish in her mouth. I parted the netting slightly to enable her to finish her job and followed her into the kitchen. After that, she managed the other dishes on her own. Once she realised that the net would not compromise her safety, she was free to execute her duties with her usual panache!

This functional character is more susceptible to trauma as they internalise and absorb everything, rather like some people who worry excessively or play things over and over in their mind. However, the amount to which an individual Guide is affected may vary due to age, gender and environment. Here is an example of internalised trauma:

An angry, intoxicated owner beats their Guide puppy. Their anger creates a heightened level of adrenaline, which has a strong scent. The puppy has absorbed the trauma of this event, and the smell of adrenaline and alcohol have become 'triggers'. The environment and odours have been filed deep in the memory banks of the puppy.

An understanding and knowledgeable new owner rehomes the puppy from a rescue centre, but must instruct visitors to their home not to attend a gym or have alcohol for 48 hours beforehand. The odours of both alcohol and adrenaline have become lifelong triggers for this Guide, who would instantly attack. This example has been taken from two true stories.

Although a Guide has a relatively large personal space 'bubble', they do not like this space invaded, unless it is on their terms. The human actions of hugging and kissing can, therefore, be stressful for them. The best way to touch your Guide is to let them approach *you* and come into *your* personal space. I have never been able to kiss or hug my Guide. I respect her personal space and the individual she is and allow her to approach me if she wants a few minutes of togetherness.

As with all canines, a Guide shows their anxiety of your invasion of their space by using 'calming signals'. They may turn their head away, yawn, lick their lips, or display 'whale' eyes – this is when a dog's eyes become very wide, and the white parts extremely visible. However, if all these subtle signals are ignored, they would enhance their 'request' for a person to move away by progressing up the 'Ladder of Aggression' (see below) until the person paid attention.

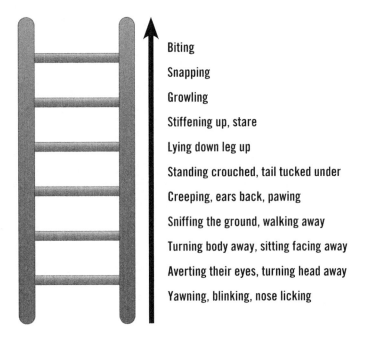

Biting

Snapping

Growling

Stiffening up, stare

Lying down leg up

Standing crouched, tail tucked under

Creeping, ears back, pawing

Sniffing the ground, walking away

Turning body away, sitting facing away

Averting their eyes, turning head away

Yawning, blinking, nose licking

Dr Kendal Shepherd BVSc., CCAB, MRCVS, created the 'Ladder of Aggression' in 2001, and it can be found in the centre pages of her book *The Canine Commandments* (see www.kendal shepherd.com/books/the-canine-commandments). Dr Shepherd is one of the UK's leading behavioural consultants and is a certified clinical animal behaviourist. Her new book *Demystifying Dog Behaviour* will be published in early 2021. www.kendal shepherd.com/books/demystifying-dog-behaviour-for-the-veterinarian

Turid Rugaas's book (see Chapter 1) also covers the calming signals contained within the Ladder of Aggression.

Guides may suddenly lunge at another dog if they get too close while they are sniffing something or resting somewhere. The lunge notifies the approaching dog that they are getting too close, as it is impolite to invade the personal space of a Guide. During an assessment of a big flat coat retriever at daycare, the dog came rushing into the main creche area where my small Guide, KD, was standing. The magical bit was when the newbie suddenly realised that he was running headlong towards a Guide and slammed the brakes on!

You may have noticed that if you have a Guide in a group of dogs playing fetch with a ball, the Guide will stop short of getting involved in the 'scrum' once the ball lands. Personal safety is of paramount importance to the Guide, and they are not willing to chance getting injured. Likewise, if you throw an article into an area of bush, a Guide may stand back and let another dog in the group go for it. This reluctance to dive into the bush also demonstrates their self-preserving nature. It is brilliant to see!

Food source is important for Guides as they need to have a more pungent personal scent than the rest of their social group. For this reason, in undomesticated social groups, Guides will head for the adrenaline-saturated parts of a 'kill', for example, wings and thighs. These body parts were still moving when the creature died and so will be full of adrenaline. Tripe, an organ meat, neutralises other meats, and therefore the way the dog smells to other dogs. So tripe could be fed to other individuals in the group, but not the Guide. Without a more pungent scent than other individuals, Guides lose their primary way to signal that they are a priority individual, which is scent.

4 Lone Individual

Lone, or Solitary, Individuals, can often be mistaken for Guides as they are also aloof and socially isolated. Like the Guide, these functional characters tend to have small social networks and big personal space bubbles that are to be entered on their terms only. Although Lone Individuals may mingle with their social group from time to time, they do prefer to be alone and will spend much of their time on the periphery of the group. Some people may try to encourage inclusion, but these characters are not usually keen on group games or snuggling up together.

Some puppies may be born as Lone Individuals, and thus found within a litter, or we can create them. For example, a single puppy in a litter could well be a Lone Individual, although not always. And a dog that lives alone with their human guardian is likely to become one – although in this situation you may not see the 'loner' characteristic of a true Lone Individual. What you will see, however, is their need to adapt, and adopt the functions of other functional characters when the only dog in a home.

However, you can begin to see the actual functional character of a dog living alone once the dog is in a more secure group environment, such as when another dog is added to the home. Another situation that would give them the safety to exhibit their authentic self would be when they are interacting with other dogs, such as on a walk or at daycare. In these situations, you will begin to see your dog's real functional character because they no longer need to adopt all functions – peacekeeping, defending, etc. I have known an overprotective owner who sadly always kept their rescue dog away from other dogs. This canine individual showed the characteristics of a Lone Individual, although I suspect now that it was a Follower.

Likewise, other functional characters, when on their own, can sometimes display the traits of another character, depending on the situation, scenario or task at hand. Dogs living alone on the streets are likely to show characteristics of other functional characters. For example, these individuals will have had to 'guide' or 'defend' themselves, and may even have had to keep the peace between other individuals on occasion. With this in mind, it could be somewhat confusing when trying to determine their character.

Lone Individuals are generally not tactile unless they feel unwell or require comfort for some reason. The love of touchy-feely is, mostly, the domain of the lovely Follower functional characters, who enjoy close contact with their owners at any time! Lone Individuals are not fond of being picked up and carried about. At my daycare we have a lovely small dog who is a Lone Individual, and she most definitely does not take kindly to being picked up. Here is an example of a non-touchy-feely Lone Individual – it is the story of my little terrier, nicknamed 'The Shark'!

The Shark

At the age of nine weeks, Gizmo, a Patterdale/Border Collie cross, attended week one of a puppy course with his owner. As the lady stood in front of me holding on to this little black bundle, he thrashed about in her arms. As soon as I looked at him, he snapped towards me and nearly fell. She said that he had bitten her seven-year-old daughter as she picked him up to cuddle him. During that first training session, he was unable to focus, and the lady became very discouraged. My advice was for short, fun training sessions during the week, with her and her daughter. I also advised her not to let her daughter pick him up because that would surely lead to another bite, which would cause more trauma for both the puppy and the child. In addition, I suggested that she fed him something other than the hyperactivity-inducing kibble he was currently eating.

The second week the lady returned and was adamant that the pup had to be rehomed as he had bitten her daughter again when she picked him up. She wanted to get rid of him before they went on holiday the following week! I suggested taking him in for a month and doing some desensitising, training and socialising. Hopefully, when they got back from their holiday, things would be vastly improved. If not, I said I would help her rehome him. To this she agreed.

We met up at a service station to transfer the pup, still in his crate, from her vehicle to mine. I had asked her to attach a puppy training line and leave him in his cage to spare him the trauma of being handled. As I lifted the tiny crate from her car boot to the front of my van, my face was quite close to the bars. So too were his teeth! He was probably the most unhappy and scared little dog that I had seen in many years, and he repeatedly tried to bite me through the cage.

Over the next two days, Gizmo stayed in his crate and watched me and the rest of my social group go about our lives. I kept the puppy training line hanging outside the cage and used this to lead him out for an emptying, and short walks throughout the day. Nobody interacted with him for two days, apart from the odd sniff of his cage on the way to the back door. On the third morning, when I took him out for an empty, the little pup jumped up my leg. I bent down and gave him a tiny piece of cheese and asked him if we were friends now. After this moment, he visibly relaxed. We had won his trust because nobody got in his space. From then on, I left the cage door open so that he was free to come and go as he wanted. Mostly he could be found in his little den, doing his own thing with a toy, or just watching everyone else.

I did loads of short training sessions with him – mostly fun things, nothing too serious, except the recall. During his time with us, we went to a few dog training demonstrations that I had been booked to do, and he was happy to participate for a few moments. The cherry on the cake for me was when he was comfortable enough to meet with a small group of children. He was happily moving from lap to lap and allowed the children to stroke him along his back.

Just two weeks into their holiday, the owner rang me to say that they had had a family meeting and had decided not to take Gizmo back when they returned. Despite his tremendous achievements with meeting and greeting, she was still adamant that they did not want him back. Then she announced, 'We want you to have him'! I informed her that I already had four dogs and was not looking to add to my group, but I would help her rehome him. The family was not happy about this arrangement, which I felt was unfair on both me and the pup. However, I later agreed to take him on as they were adamant they didn't want him back. I thought it might be possible for me to rehome him myself further down the line.

That was back in 2013. Eight years on, Gizmo has changed his name to Wizzi (aka 'The Shark'!) and is still with me. He is still precious about his personal space, but that's just who is. I organise and manage his life to avoid him ever being put in a situation that he cannot handle. I have never been able to hug or kiss this little dog, and I never try – I respect who he is and his personal space requirements. Towelling him down after a muddy walk makes him cross, but he has learnt to accept me doing this and diligently gives me each paw on cue for drying off.

I knew nothing of functional characters when I first decided to keep Wizzi – I just knew I had a dog that had been pushed to the limit and needed to learn to trust. I believe that Wizzi made the journey to the top of the 'Ladder of Aggression' much more quickly due to him being a Lone Individual. Through no fault of his own, he had ended up at the top of the 'ladder'. If his original family had taken the time to understand and read his calming signals, he might still be with them now.

Even though I manage his life for him, there are times when this falls apart. Because he is quite cute, he is a bit of a people magnet, and at times I've had to warn folk not to approach or touch him or he will bite. Those who have ignored me have suffered the consequences of his weaponry making contact with their skin. These situations are irritating because they confirm to Wizzi that he should indeed mistrust humans. My other concern at such times is that these people create the possibility of his bite moving further up the Dunbar Bite Scale – see www.dogstardaily. com/training/bite-scale

So, as we've seen, having a large personal space bubble may mean the Lone Individual will not be the sort of puppy that takes well to being picked up and cuddled.

In my experience of Lone Individuals thus far, I have found them to be easy enough to train. However, we must bear in mind the breed predispositions of the individual. Also, previous training history should be considered for older or rescue dogs, because everything plays a part in the dog we see before us.

Because of the solitary nature of this functional character, we can run into similar problems that may occur with a Guide, due to their independence. Also, a terrier-type with personal space issues lunging at another dog can look more aggressive than a Labrador, for example. Likewise, if you have one of the 'feared' large breeds and it springs towards another dog, do not wait around for the verbal abuse. Having been the proud owner of many Rottweilers, I feel that pain!

Depending on the early life of the Lone Individual puppy, if another dog gets too close to them while they are sniffing something, they may simply growl. Alternatively, they may launch a noisy 'assault' on them. Again, this is where breed pre-dispositions need to be taken into account. For example, a Lone Individual terrier mix with a stressful start in life is going to be a vastly different character to a Cavalier King Charles Spaniel brought up in a calm and understanding home. By understanding your Lone Individual's needs, you will be more able to steer them through any situation while helping them stay calm.

Beyond the Breed

As a final note, Dr Isla Fishburn shared with me that many people ask her how you can tell the difference between a Guide and a Lone Individual. Her reply has been set out in the table below, which hopefully makes the difference easier to see.

GUIDE	LONE INDIVIDUAL
They are only interested in what *they* want to do...	
... although they are interested in what the group are doing by way of checking in on them.	... with no need to keep a close connection to the rest of the group.

5 Defender

This functional character is known as an Enforcer, Defender or Protector, as its role is all three of these. They are strong and confident, and are by far the most substantial individuals in a litter. There can be more than one born, particularly in a larger litter. Defenders can be either sex, although females are less common. Because of their bulk, a female Defender would look very masculine. They are sturdy, strong and confident, and are the natural defenders in, and of a social group. Although some Followers can be the biggest in a litter, the Defender is noticeably sturdier. The confidence of a Follower can often equal that of a Defender, though the latter has more confidence in its desire to explore. This confidence can often be seen as boisterous behaviour due to the relatively upbeat attitude of a typical Defender. This boisterousness would be exacerbated in breeds that are predisposed to be somewhat enthusiastic!

The Defender is a good problem-solver and mentally more able to deal with situations that other functional characters would find scary or traumatic. They bring strength through confidence and are the characters more likely to put themselves forward and in front of what might be perceived as a threat to the group. A 'threat' could include a person or another dog or, in an undomes-ticated group, anything that threatens the safety of the group.

Their other role is that of Enforcer – they 'enforce' the rules of correct and fair discipline that they were taught in early life. This early learning could be from either a canine or a human, depending on whether the dog is domesticated or not. Although, of course, a youngster could be taught by another canine even in a domestic environment. Here are two examples of protecting and enforcing.

Defender A

This puppy is owned by a young couple who have a friend who advised them to smack it when it gets too boisterous. Then the couple have a baby and initially the pup, now an adolescent, and the baby are inseparable. The dog protects the baby by lying close by and keeping the human puppy warm. However, things change when the child starts moving around on its own and becomes overexcited. The dog now becomes an Enforcer. It enforces the rules it was taught as a pup by its Guides – the owners, i.e. boisterous behaviour is physically admonished. Because the dog cannot smack, it bites the child to stop it from being so rowdy.

Defender B

Getting too boisterous with a sibling is admonished by the pup's canine mother by being picked up and moved away from the litter. In this way, the puppy has been denied warmth. Warmth is one of the primary needs of a young animal – it provides safety and security, as well as a sense of belonging. Being denied this essential need is quite a punishment for a young pup, but in a way that is not harmful or traumatic and allows for a balanced learning of correction. Given the same situation as Defender A, this dog would admonish the child's boisterous activity by moving away from them, thus denying them warmth.

From the above examples, we can see that chastisement has been meted out according to the approach used when they were young.

Defenders do tend to be very exuberant in their play and meeting and greeting behaviours. They are very gung-ho, and likely to be one of the first pups to say 'hi' when you visit a litter. A Staffordshire Bull Terrier Defender would be like a thrill-seeker on steroids! On a serious note, though, it is possible to see why this breed, and character, could potentially get themselves into trouble. I have a female Staffie/Labrador who is a Defender. Born in August 2016, she has been attending my daycare facility every day since she was nine weeks old and is an extremely confident individual. Her method of play is often rough, which is typical of this functional character – playmates are carefully chosen to avoid problems.

When socialising a young Defender, the same rule applies – use the more social functional characters such as Peacekeeper, Follower or Hunter, but who are social individuals themselves. Socialising at puppy parties can often end badly for Defenders, particularly if there are several of them at the same gathering. Presenting them with something or someone new would not cause hesitation, and their natural exuberance can be a little daunting for first-time dog owners.

When training, Defenders can cope with lots of repetition, and they are great problem-solvers. However, training can sometimes fall apart when they are out in public. In her online course (https://kachinacanine.com/online-course), Dr Isla Fishburn recounts her visit to a lady with a German Shepherd Defender. The lady in question competed with her Shepherd at the highest levels of competition obedience, and her dog was impeccably well trained. However, first place kept eluding the pair, and the owner could not work out why. His heel position was precisely where he needed to be at training classes, but at competitions he would move marginally forward. Dr Isla advised the owner that he would move ahead to 'protect' his Guide due to being male, and a Defender functional character. Competitions naturally make us nervous and so the change in her biochemistry, coupled with lots of activity in the competition area, caused the Defender's characteristics to override his impeccable ability to remain in the heel position. A Defender that is also a German Shepherd gives us a double dose of protector!

In terms of fresh food feeding, the food source is unimportant to a Defender. They are not concerned that their bodily scent is less pungent than that of their Guide. However, if tension or conflict arises between a Defender and another functional character in the home, feeding more muscle meat to the Defender can balance out the intensity between the two individuals.

As a final note on this chapter, it is *never* a good idea to physically discipline a dog or puppy. In the dog world, early learning and correction are done so as not to traumatise an individual. Canine etiquette taught in a canine-only environment is firm and fair and allows for a balanced education.

6 Observer

The Observer is a shy and nervous individual, suspicious and wary of new things, and their need for safety can border on neurotic. Their role in a social group is to look out for potential danger while the group is busy – they do this by listening and looking, but also by using scent. A rustle in the bushes or a slight change in odour in the air, and the Observer will erupt into rapid-fire barking to get the group's attention. All of this helps to explain why they are quite scatty!

I describe these characters as life's worrywarts due to their over-anxious and insecure nature. Like the Overseer, the Observer thrives on routine and likes a calm environment. The reason is that it gives them fewer situations in which they need to be vigilant and alert the group. It's not a good idea to breed from these characters because they produce nervous and suspicious puppies, irrespective of the functional characters of the pups. In a non-domestic environment, the Observer would not be a breeding individual.

Observers are frequently confused with Guides as they are both 'shy'. When viewing a litter of puppies, here's a way you may be able to tell a Guide from an Observer. Like a Guide, the Observer will most likely be at the back, keeping its distance. However, *unlike* a Guide, the Observer may often look petrified. Guides are very majestic and would probably not even glance up at a person entering the room. Instead, they would be watching their littermates to see what happens to them. The Observer puppy is often picked ahead of other pups in the litter due to it gazing up at a potential new owner with those classic puppy-dog eyes! The reason for their shy demeanour is because they are naturally suspicious of all new things and people, and would be wary the moment anyone walked into the room.

Observers need lots of socialising and desensitising, *but* this should be done at a snail's pace to help build their confidence. This character needs lots of time, care and attention, but not in a mollycoddling sort of way. For example, picking them up and rocking them in your arms like a baby will do nothing to lessen or resolve their anxiety at any given time. We can support them by going out with them for a last-minute wee at night, as they would struggle with being shut outside alone. Being alone in the garden soaking up all the noises would not only make them severely anxious, but also unable to toilet. Once back indoors where they feel safe, they will then empty themselves, which is not conducive to speedy house training! Toileting leaves any dog vulnerable to 'attack' because they are stationary, but more importantly it 'advertises' who they are. A dog that is fearful of its surroundings would not want to leave its scent by toileting.

The spring and summer months are best for socialising and desensitising all functional characters, but particularly the Observer. These times of the year give us longer hours of daylight and none of the spooky shadows seen in the half-light of autumn and winter! To be able to slow down their learning sufficiently, it would be best to take an Observer for as many short adventures each day as possible, giving them time for exploration and confidence building.

Observers are likely to be barkers and are also prone to separation issues. Fearful, anxious dogs are generally more nervous when home alone because the doorway you went out of is easily big enough for a large predator to get through. A Guide living as an only dog may also have this fear because there are no group members to stand in front of them and 'protect' them. Dogs have no way of knowing that only family or friends will come in through the door, or that you'll be home in a short while. As soon as you go out and close the door behind you, the Observer feels unsafe. To a dog, the size of the exit is big enough for something scary to enter and, as we have already discussed, safety is the primary need of every dog.

Observers are fearful of new things, and may panic or become suspicious if:

➤ a piece of furniture is moved from one place, or one room, to another

➤ your handbag is left on a different part of the kitchen counter

➤ you pop open a 'blister' pack of treats or tablets

➤ your stomach rumbles while they are snuggling with you on the sofa

➤ you get out or put up the ironing board

➤ a road sign or dustbin has been left on the pavement that wasn't there the last time they walked along that street.

These are just a few of the things that owners of Observers have told me. One owner says that her Border Collie Observer doesn't have a problem if she comes downstairs with piles of washing in her arms, but if she is carrying ironing, he runs and hides! The scent of the clean clothing may be the trigger because it is associated with the ironing board coming out of the cupboard.

Another problem that may be encountered with an Observer is a reluctance to leave the house for a walk. Although this is more likely in a single-dog household, it could happen in a multi-dog home. When helping owners in the past, I've advised them to leave a trail of extra-tasty treats over the threshold. Many of them told me that this didn't make any difference – one of them even tried lying down on the doormat to coax their puppy out of the door. Now that I understand the importance of functional characters, and exactly why an Observer doesn't want to go out, my advice is quite different.

Walking an Observer with a Defender would give them confidence and emotional support. That's all very well you might say, but how do I find a Defender? Our Beyond the Breed functional character workshops have been put together to assist us in becoming more proficient at determining functional characters. However, if you cannot attend a workshop for any reason, this book will hopefully go some way to helping you.

Try to study as many dogs and their interactions as you can and look at dogs that live near you. Speak with their guardians and if you feel their dog is a Defender or perhaps even a Guide, ask them to come and meet you at your home. Naturally, it's important to ensure that both dogs are dog friendly. Maybe meet in your back garden at first, and see if your dog wants to explore the outside world further now they have a Defender with them. I know this has worked to great effect in the past.

If you already have an Observer and are thinking of getting another dog, consider a Defender, a Guide, or even a Follower.

Overseer

Overseers are the eccentrics of the dog world but, as with all functional characters, they have a role to play within a social group. These intense characters can create chaos, within groups and households alike, due to their manic and obsessive behaviours. As puppies, Overseers can nip a lot, but can also be very appeasing, and are often described as having ADHD or labelled 'untrainable'. However, they are often quite bright individuals and, if placed in the right role, they can indeed excel.

These functional characters need to know that everything is safe. They ask for, and promote, calm within their social group. Once the group is calm, an Overseer can relax. They ask for calm by nipping, also known as testing. They seek confirmation that all individuals in the group are fit for their functional purpose each day. In essence, they are the canine equivalent of a quality assurance manager! Their testing behaviour helps to ensure the safety and survival of the group. For example, suppose a Defender is not up to their job one day – who will protect and defend the group? The testing (nipping), is perhaps easier to understand if put in conversation form, and this might be one between an Overseer and a Defender:

Overseer   'Are you okay to defend and protect us today?'

Defender   'Yes.'

Overseer   'Are you really sure?'

Defender	'Yes!'
Overseer	'Absolutely sure?'
Defender	'Yeesss!'
Overseer	'Completely positive?'
Defender	'How many times do I need to tell you?!'
Overseer	'Well, you know, yesterday you hurt your paw, and I need to check that you can defend, protect and enforce today.'
Defender	'Well, I'm absolutely up to the job today, so go away!'

The way the Defender would make this last comment is by one very deliberate, self-assured and quite abrupt communication, terminating the Overseer's testing. In this way, the Defender has physically proven that they are up to the task of enforcing and protecting, giving the Overseer absolute proof. I would add here that, for first-time dog owners and novice professionals, the Defender's communication could easily be mistaken for 'aggression'. The downside of anyone stepping in to break up this essential piece of canine communication is that it can cause frustration in the relationship between the individuals in the future.

So, now the Overseer has their 'feedback', they move on and test (quality assure) the next individual in the group. If an individual is unwell or has been injured, the testing might become obsessive, as in the above 'conversation'. An Overseer's restlessness that the individual may not be fit for their role on a given day manifests as obsessive behaviour, bordering on mania. If you have multiple dogs and one of them is an Overseer, be aware that you may see some neurotic behaviour if another individual has an injury.

Another obsessive behaviour exhibited by Overseers is irrational barking. They often bark at their owner or another dog, or even at nothing. Persistently hanging off their lead is a fixation that many Overseers have, and so teaching lead walking is often troublesome. Despite having received feedback from other members of their social group, repeated 'testing' is another of the Overseer's intense behaviours. However, all this assumes that the Overseer is fed a fresh food, raw diet. Individuals who consume processed food that contains 'cereals' can be excessively hyperactive due to the unhealthy ingredients in the food.

> 'Guides are mentally challenging to own, Defenders are physically challenging to own, and Overseers are both!'
>
> – DR ISLA FISHBURN

Overseers may also challenge other functional characters, including the Guide, to test their ability to function as that particular character. They may steal food from the Guide to 'test' them, and when they get promptly disciplined, they have their feedback! Disciplining can range from a snap or lunge right up to an Overseer being slammed onto the floor. All of this can look quite scary for new dog owners, or those who are somewhat anthropomorphic with their view of dogs.

The Overseer's manic, testing behaviour starts with the disproportionate nipping they demonstrate as puppies. This type of nipping would be in addition to the biting that puppies display when they are trying to learn bite inhibition, i.e. how hard is too hard. An Overseer, then, can seem like an excessive biter, in addition to being a puppy that never seems to learn how to inhibit their bite.

There may not be an Overseer in every litter, but if there is, it's usually only one. When you visit a breeder to choose your puppy, you may see testing behaviour from almost any individual in the litter as they play and tumble around. However, if a puppy is hanging off the curtains, you can be fairly sure it's an Overseer!

Usually, there is never a dull moment when you have an Overseer in the house. Some owners have said that they behave like severely autistic children. The Overseer individual would undoubtedly pose a real challenge for a first-time dog owner. The intense nature of this functional character can make them problematic to train and socialise, and both they and their owners would benefit from a tailored approach to these. Overseers are not the sort of puppies that can just be lumped into a large puppy training group. They may need to be kept busy in between practical exercises to avoid frustrated behaviours such as shouting and nipping. The same rule would apply to classes for adult dogs too. Teaching an Overseer is, for the most part, not an easy job. Frustration can quickly set in if they struggle to grasp the task involved, and if this happens, we must be prepared to show them a different way to learn something. One owner of an Overseer told me, 'Repetition wasn't enjoyable once the task had been learned. He got frustrated if we didn't move on to something else fast enough.' The Overseer's exasperation is similar to that of a Guide, but more intense and 'shouty'.

We need to stay serene and unflustered during training sessions with these guys to help them stay focused and less flighty. Training sessions are best done little and often, and be prepared to start each new session with a reasonably lengthy recap from the last one! Or prepare to marvel at your Overseer returning to the spot from where the previous session ended, because they do often surprise us!

Because Overseers are there to promote and ask for calm, they are best suited to a quiet household with as much routine as possible to help them thrive. High-energy homes would fuel the Overseer's functional purpose – they would become more panicky, making them test more. Fewer situations to 'test' are afforded by a quiet lifestyle with plenty of routine – this also provides Overseers with confirmation that everything is 'safe'. A relaxed owner and environment denote, on the whole, a relaxed Overseer.

Dr Isla Fishburn tells us that Overseers 'highlight any changes in biochemistry, and teach us about having an awareness of this'. From this perspective, an Overseer may well be an excellent choice to train as a medical alert dog. Training for this type of role would play to the Overseer's strength, even though they don't have the problem-solving skills of the Guide or Defender.

However, as with all dogs, and all functional characters, they are individuals. What suits one dog or person may not be to someone else's taste.

When assessing an Overseer, they can sometimes be confused with an Observer as they can also be very scatty. Observers need a quiet home with plenty of routine, just like the Overseer, but for a different reason. The Overseer needs routine to have fewer situations in which to test, and the Observer needs a quiet home with a routine to give them more reasons to feel safe. Things that might cause panic for an Observer, and testing in an Overseer, are, for example:

➤ a piece of furniture being moved from one place, or room, to another

➤ a bag being left on a different part of the kitchen counter to where it is usually placed.

These may cause an Overseer to 'test' because they are different to normal, and the Overseer is asking 'Why is this different?'

The main difference between the Overseer and the Observer is the intensity of their behaviours. Those of the Overseer are over-enthusiastic and, like fruit juice – concentrated! An Observer may appear weird and wacky at times, but the Overseer takes this to the extreme. When fed on a fresh food, natural raw diet, the true characteristics of the Overseer should be visible. Processed food can 'mask' these characteristics, and do not aid in giving a clear indication as to whether or not you share your life and your home with an Overseer.

I recently asked the members of my private Facebook group 'If you have more than one dog, including an Overseer, how has the presence of the Overseer affected (or not) the other individuals in the group?' Here is an interesting reply from a lady whose group comprises three large breeds – a male Follower, a female Peacekeeper and a male Overseer.

'I had the Follower first, then the Overseer, followed by a Peacekeeper. When the Overseer came home, the Follower took him under his wing. He looks after him all the time,

and when he gets too high, he flattens him. However, he also lets him get away with murder! I love the little bond they have. The Overseer didn't impact on the Peacekeeper at all when she came, and they play a lot together. He has settled dramatically, and is less testy with the presence of the Peacekeeper.'

I've always believed that dogs come into our life for a reason. And so, if you currently live with an Overseer, give thanks for the patience and additional skills that this scatty individual will bring you.

8 Peacekeeper

The Peacekeeper functional character is a significant individual in a social group. Their job is to encourage peace when bickering or tension between individuals looks likely. They act like a referee during play but, more importantly, diffuse and break up arguments by redirecting attention onto themselves. They do this by getting in between quarrelling individuals, or by whimpering or barking.

'The Overseer creates bickering, and the Peacekeeper is at the hands of all the bickering.'

– Dr Isla Fishburn

Peacekeepers seem to be always 'monitoring' their environment for tension. They can speedily and efficiently move from playing with one individual to racing across the room to deal with a potential issue arising between other individuals. At my daycare facility, we've also seen Observers go from a snoozing position in one of the dog beds to racing across the room to halt the game of some others playing. On these occasions it's more a case of the Observer wanting to quell the high energy of the dogs playing, rather than them taking on a Peacekeeper role. Although some dogs are true Peacekeepers, other functional characters may present this role if there is no true Peacekeeper in the group.

A peacekeeping method I've observed from a Follower and a Defender, as well as a Peacekeeper, is the muzzle 'punch'. In addition to being an energy diffuser, this behaviour is also about potential unbalance in group composition at the time. Peacekeepers may be mistaken for Defenders when deploying a muzzle punch, due to the full-on nature of the behaviour. However, as mentioned in the Defender chapter, these are much bulkier individuals than Peacekeepers. PLEASE NOTE: A muzzle punch is an accepted dog-to-dog communication method within an established group. *Under no circumstances should a dog be punched by a human.*

When energy levels increase between people, during a heated discussion, say, a Peacekeeper may walk into the group and draw attention to themselves. They do this to break things up and calm the energy of the individuals involved. You may have noticed this if you have a Peacekeeper and you quarrel with someone else at home. It can also happen during an argument with someone on the phone – your Peacekeeper may come close to you and whimper or bark.

Peacekeepers are very caring and supportive individuals and, like the Followers, are quite sensitive souls. As puppies, Peacekeepers are very appeasing and licky, and would spend a lot of time on their back when playing. Being on their back is another technique they use to draw the heat out of tension between other puppies in the litter. Confusingly, most puppies in a litter spend time on their back when playing. However, the more you study the pups, the more you will notice that a Peacekeeper spends an excessive amount of time on their back.

Adult Peacekeepers are great individuals to have around when introducing puppies to older dogs. However, we do need to ensure that they are well-socialised individuals themselves. As we saw in the previous chapter, Peacekeepers have a calming influence on an Overseer in the same social group.

 **9 Follower**

Followers love being handled and are affable and affec-
tionate characters who welcome closeness and attention. They
appreciate physical support – touching and stroking, which is
an excellent way to confirm that they are doing well. However,
it can be a fine line between supportive touching and excessive
physical contact. Given their more dependent nature, Followers,
and some other functional characters, can be more prone to
suffer from separation distress on some level. As with all dogs,
separation distress can be prevented by not treating a dog like a
human baby or small child, thus enabling them to learn to feel
safe and confident indoors on their own. It is possible, though,
for separation issues to happen dog to dog as well as dog to
person. For example, in a multi-dog household, how many times
have we heard of, or seen, a dog suddenly develop separation
distress after a human or dog member of their family passes
away? Or where a dog may show separation distress when dog
A is taken out of the home, yet no separation distress if dog B
is taken out? A Guide or Defender would help other functional
characters with separation distress by providing more stability
and comfort.

Typically, Followers are greedy with their food and very oppor-
tunistic around it – a trait usually only attributed to Labradors!
Followers also need a lot more encouragement than Defenders
or Guides, which is one way you can tell these three functional
characters apart.

In general, larger litters contain more than one Follower, and their confidence level, and size, will vary. The larger and more confident Followers could be mistaken for Defenders as they are often similarly built. However, on closer inspection, you will see the differences:

FOLLOWER	DEFENDER
Range of sizes	One size – large
Larger ones can be big boned	Bulky, with a considerably bigger physique
Range in confidence	Mostly, highly confident[1]
Not as willing to explore	All are willing to explore
Less likely to go far from the owner when out on a walk	More likely to be off doing their own thing when out on a walk
A bit of a lazybones!	Will laze as required
Easy to teach due to love of food	Can tolerate much longer training sessions
Speed of learning varies, but requires more repetitions over many sessions to learn	Very quick to learn and can tolerate many repetitions in one session
Loves being handled and touched	Ditto, but not as demanding
Not designed for problem-solving	Good problem-solver

[1] An Observer bitch is likely to produce unconfident Defenders

Followers have a less gung-ho attitude than Defenders, preferring to wait for instruction. Because of this they are quite lazy (on standby), with an attitude of 'call me if you need me'! Essentially, this laid-back attitude is because Followers are the reinforcements, the reserves – on standby until needed. They support other characters with protecting, hunting and looking out for potential danger, etc. If a Follower sees that another individual in their group needs help, they go to assist. However, they can sometimes go in with guns blazing and create conflict which may not have arisen had they not got involved. A Follower does not necessarily need to live with the dog to whom it offers support – it may be a dog that it walks with or meets on a walk. Equally, it may be an individual it knows from its neighbourhood or a local dog park. At my daycare facility, we have seen a Follower offering support to another dog that it knows only from daycare.

Their love of food makes a Follower easy to train, although they can take quite a long time to learn things. This slow learning ability is because they cannot tolerate too many repetitions in a training session. During the training process, you may have to do a recap for them many times, and you may have to go back a stage or two at the beginning of each session. You may often see a little expression on their face that says, 'Could you run that by me one more time please?'! However, once they have got it, you are good to go. If you teach your Follower something that you then only ask them to do once a week, do not be surprised if they forget how to do it!

Followers would mostly not reproduce in a social group, but obviously it is different in a domestic environment. Breeding with these individuals is not as big an issue as it would be with an Observer. However, it may not be a great idea to breed with a Follower who is at the very timid end of the scale.

Whether you are a dog owner or work with dogs, if you run a group that includes an entire Follower and a neutered Guide, you may well find that the former gets a hard time from the latter. Long ago, the advice I received was always to neuter the *least* dominant dog to preserve the position of the 'alpha' or most dominant dog. However, I now know that that is not the best option. Also, I no longer use the word 'dominant' as I believe it does nothing to explain the dynamics between individuals. With our understanding of functional characters, we can now get neutering right every time, helping our social group thrive, rather than just tolerate each other. I would add that I am not in favour of wholesale neutering – it is down to individual circumstances.

I love the account Dr Isla Fishburn gives in her Complete Canine Wellness course of her time working with wolves, when a Follower wolf ate liver after a kill. Organ meat is not an appropriate food source for a Follower and for two days afterwards, he would empty himself in the water trough to disguise his pungent smell. However, the scent was also shed from his coat, and he was subsequently admonished, not by the Guide, but by the Defender! What a great illustration of how important scent is to canines.

Followers who are more physically and mentally robust may make excellent protection dogs, police dogs or assistance dogs, such as those trained to help people who are blind. Less self-confident individuals may be excellent helper dogs or therapy dogs, given the right socialising, desensitisation and training. The type of assistance dogs trained by the charity Dog AID, for example, would also suit a more timid Follower.

# 10 Hunter

The Latin name for the group that our domesticated dog comes under is *Canis lupus familiaris*. It is a sub-species of wolf – *Canis lupus*. Individually, the word meanings are:

Canis – dog (the family)

lupus – wolf

familiaris – domestic

Dogs are domesticated mammals from the Canidae family, and of the order Carnivora. All individuals under the Carnivora order have specialised over millions of years to primarily consume meat. They are predators, and all predators hunt.

When examining our Hunter functional character within a social group, these individuals are the natural hunters. They are also known as Pursuers.

The Hunter functional character is a whippet-like individual – fast and agile, and extremely focused on anything that moves. If you visit a litter with a Hunter puppy in it, look out for the one who's the most focused on anything that moves, long after the others have forgotten about it and nodded off! The reason for this is that watching for movement is an integral part of being a good hunter. If you suspect you have a Hunter puppy in your litter, you can determine it quite easily using a sock, cloth or fleecy toy when the pups are settling down. Twitch the toy around swiftly in the air, a few feet away from the litter – all except a Hunter will find it challenging to stay focused on the movement. The Hunter will be mesmerised.

Hunters are great working individuals and are up for lots of repetition. Like Defenders, they are easy to train, and can cope with long training sessions – much more than we would do with our Followers, Overseers or Observers, for example. Gun dog people have told me that they are one of the best functional characters to train as gun dogs, which is brilliant because it plays to their strengths. Because a Spaniel has been bred to be a natural working dog, one who is also a Hunter functional character would surely be the ultimate 'hunter', or gun dog. However, sometimes the instincts of the Hunter can be hard to moderate for a dog that you want to have a soft mouth, retrieve game, or only chase on cue.

Hunters are not overly afraid and have a tremendously high prey drive. Those who own sighthounds that are also Hunter functional characters may find this double dose of prey drive quite over-whelming at times. Desensitising from day one helps with this, although I know there will always be individuals that can't be let off the lead. The earlier a Hunter puppy starts training and desensitising to movement, the better.

Like our Observer functional character, it can be hard to keep weight on a Hunter, and they may always look underfed. Due to their lean physique, male Hunters do look quite feminine. To help gain a little weight, some people give their Hunter a small meal of tripe meat right before bedtime.

11 Nanny/Guardian

This character cannot be identified in a litter as it is only seen in an adolescent or older dog. They are very balanced characters who are good teachers, and only a few adults will display the nurturing behaviour of a Nanny/Guardian. If you have an old dog in the house who really perks up when a new puppy is brought home, your 'oldie' will likely be a Nanny/Guardian.

In a household with multiple dogs and a bitch who is pregnant, you may see puppy-type behaviours from some of the rest of the group. From these individuals, the bitch will decide who she will need to keep away from her pups once born, and who will have access to them from the beginning. The Nanny/Guardian chosen by the pregnant bitch could even be an Overseer, which was the case for a friend of mine whose bitch had puppies in 2019.

A Nanny/Guardian would be one of the best functional characters to socialise with young individuals. A good understanding of functional characters would be of enormous benefit to those running large puppy gatherings, particularly if they can invite a Nanny/Guardian to each event. In the initial stages, it would probably be best to split puppies into groups, maybe as follows:

Gung-ho Let's Go!	Don't Rush Me!
Overseers	Guides
Defenders	Observers
More confident Followers	Less confident Followers
Hunters	Lone Individuals
Peacekeepers	Peacekeepers
	Hunters

The reason for adding Peacekeepers and Hunters to both lists is because they could fit into either group. Whenever we have a large number of dogs at my daycare facility, we split them into these groups, which helps to ensure that quieter characters are not overwhelmed by more exuberant ones. The dogs often split themselves up naturally, although knowing their functional characters does allow us to make this a more controlled separation, thus giving the quieter dogs a better experience.

My suggestion is that the groups are not mixed until the 'puppy party' organiser is happy with the way both groups are running. Run by a functional character-savvy person, these 'parties' can be extremely beneficial for all dogs and owners. Owners of the more energetic puppies can be given individual advice on socialising and training, instead of the current custom of banning their attendance altogether.

12 Characters That Complement

Knowing the functional character of our current dog, or those of our social group, benefits us by more than just day-to-day living with them. For example, when adding another individual into the mix, we:

➤ can choose an individual that will complement rather than clash with our current dog or group

➤ know that we have done our best to ensure there are no conflicts further down the line by choosing a complementing character

➤ have the ability to choose an individual that suits our lifestyle and activity level by more than just its breed.

Many people choose a new addition to their home and social group with their heart rather than head. Countless others end up owning a dog that is frequently at loggerheads with some or all of their social group, which can be stressful. It is also very time consuming and problematic to continually plan each day purely because Fido is reactive to Rover. Trying to ensure that each day runs as smoothly as possible because of problem pets can be a nightmare. But suppose we had additional knowledge to support a better-informed original decision? Knowledge that would enable our new pet to flourish and not flounder within our current social group. It would be very satisfying in the long term, to know that all will be well when we get the new addition home and, potentially, for the lifetime of all the individuals concerned.

I am not naïve enough to think that there will not be some snags along the way. As I have said in previous chapters, there are many things, over and above functional character, that need to be considered when thinking of bringing a new individual into our social group. But if we understand the fundamentals, we can strive to make things a lot more amicable than they may otherwise be. Getting relationships off on the right paw from day one would, I'm sure, help prevent so many dogs ending up at rescue centres. Let's imagine this scenario as an example:

> *Fido lives with four other dogs who will tolerate him, but he shows more conflict with and antagonises Rover. Fido is taken to the nearby rescue centre where the staff are told that Fido doesn't get along with dogs. Fido is 'assessed' before being put up for adoption. For argument's sake, let's say that Fido lunges and reacts to two of the three dogs during the assessment. The rescue centre staff decide to advertise him as 'cannot live with other dogs'. He is kept separate from other dogs while they wait for his 'forever' home.*

If this example were a real case, we would have yet another dog that most of us would be unable to rehome because we already have a dog. My question now is 'What happens when the new, possibly novice owner, tries to take Fido out for a walk or to a training class?' His reactivity is likely to be worse, having been kept on his own during his time at the rescue centre. Depending on Fido's functional character, he may well be better off living with a more experienced owner, and other dogs. For the sake of a bit of additional knowledge and understanding, Fido may now spend his life never being allowed to interact with another of his species.

Suppose Fido's functional character did not complement his original group? Remember, groups may 'expel' *any* individual superfluous to the group's needs and balance. Perhaps this is what happened to Fido when he lived with Rover and the others. Now he has ended up in rescue because of his normal and natural behaviours as the functional character he is. It is possible that, with some forward planning when purchased, Fido may have stayed with his original group. Also, if the rescue centre's evaluation of Fido had included a functional character

Suppose Fido is	Suppose another in the group was	Potential issues
An Overseer[1]	Any functional character except an Overseer	Fido's 'quality controlling' may easily be mistaken for aggression by someone not conversant with functional characters and the Overseer's role.
A Defender (female)	A Lone Individual (male)	If the Lone Individual is the only male in the group, he may be antagonised by the Defender. As the only male in the group, this would be her way of asking 'Where is your strength?' He may be physically provoked to the point where he snaps at, or even bites, the Defender. She may stand over him to force him out of a particular sleeping spot so that she can lie down there.[2]
An Observer	Any functional character except a Guide	The Observer may snap if some of the group are playing excitedly close by, because high energy does not enable an Observer to feel safe.[3]
A Lone Individual	Any functional character	Sometimes, any movement in the same room is enough to set off a grumble, or even a snap, from a Lone Individual who just wants to do their own thing.[4]

[1] This would certainly explain the bickering between him and the rest of his original social group.

[2] These are precisely the things that happen between my female Defender and my male Lone Individual, who is the only male in the group.

[3 & 4] These could easily be misinterpreted as 'aggression'.

assessment, he might have escaped the label 'cannot live with dogs', and a life of isolation and solitary living, in this hypothetical example.

However, even when we know our social group's functional characters, we may still slip up. It is not an exact science. As discussed in previous chapters, there are many other things to consider when assessing individual functional characters. Also, the interactions between certain characters can be difficult to understand at times. For example, generally Defenders are not great devotees of Overseers, and you may see some conflict between these individuals. On the other hand, you may not. Like I said, it is not an exact science!

As an example – one of the characters in my own social group is an exceptionally confident female Defender. She is a Staffie/Labrador and can be a bit exuberant at times. When she attends my daycare facility, her favourite chums are the other 'fizzy' individuals, in terms of breed, not functional character. Overseers are mostly not her cup of tea, although she is not a fan of those who lack some confidence either! On the days we have an Overseer or any less socialised or confident individual at daycare, my Defender is prevented from having close contact. Conversely, we have a 15-month-old intact male Defender that comes to daycare who is also incredibly confident, but nowhere near as gung-ho as mine in any of his interactions with other dogs. He is a Vizsla, and therefore his breed, age and gender make him a different kind of Defender to mine.

One of our loveliest little canine clients was turned away from another daycare facility, only minutes into her assessment. She has settled in brilliantly with us, although her functional character is still being assessed. Such is the power of understanding dogs at a deeper level. By fine-tuning the interactions between dogs at daycare, and with our working knowledge of functional characters, we can tailor each individual's visit and provide them with the best experience possible. All dogs can be helped; you just have to know how to personalise that help to the individual. Equally, dogs must be allowed to express themselves and communicate to others, without excessive interruption from humans. It is a fine line to draw but can be done with a deeper understanding of dogs, their functional characters, and the traits of those characters.

'Recognising a dog's functional character when understanding group composition can be useful for canine wellness and the support of an existing group.'

– DR ISLA FISHBURN

Future additions

When we get a new dog, it is tough not to buy on impulse – I understand that. I also know that it may be an impossible task to assess the functional character of every dog at the rescue centres. I'm not saying this stuff is easy, going to be easy, or that it will be a 'quick fix' to the issues of dogs not getting on with each other. We may still end up with dogs that don't suit our lifestyle or our group composition, but what I am saying is that we must try to:

➤ *Think* more carefully before we purchase a pet – consider, wherever possible, what might happen during that individual's lifetime. I know this is tricky. Several times my life has been turned upside down in an instant, presenting me with some extreme challenges. We just need to plan ahead as best we can.

➤ Choose a breed or breed type that will suit our lifestyle, family and activity level.

➤ Where possible, choose a functional character that will suit our environment, both indoors and outdoors.

➤ Train our new addition from day one. Rather than 'shake a paw', teach something more useful, such as relax and settle in a room or indoor kennel away from the family. An exercise like this will help build confidence and prevent separation issues. Recall, relax and settle on a mat or in a dog cage (indoor kennel), and accepting being touched all over (body inspection) should be the absolute minimum we teach initially. These exercises are especially important for those functional characters that might be more prone to separation anxiety or show a reluctance to being handled.

In the years to come, as we improve our functional character skills and our understanding of dogs at a much deeper level, we will be able to prolong and enrich their lives still further. However, if we find that we need to rehome a pet further down the line, we should consider more carefully where they will go. Questions to consider are:

➤ Will the new owner suit the dog and its functional character, and vice versa?

➤ What is the lifestyle and household situation of a potential new owner? For example, is it a busy home with lots of visitors and comings and goings?

➤ Will anyone in the potential new home use a shock collar on your soon-to-be ex-pet? Yes, it's horrific to have to consider this, but it does happen. Sadly, there are 'trainers' out there who do this because they know that the shock collar will give the 'quick fix' that most people want. They can then pocket a handsome fee and move on to 'zap' the next misunderstood dog. I cannot think of it without abhorrence. Dog-friendly, lasting behaviour reformation is not something that can be done overnight.

➤ Are we able to do a home check? By doing this if possible, it enables us to be relatively sure where our dog is going. I believe that some rescue centres in the UK may try to find a new home for your dog while it remains with you.

It would be brilliant if rescue centres, where possible, could rehome a dog as a functional character, instead of the monotonous 'cannot live with dogs' marker. Yes, I understand that there are, and will always be, dogs that simply cannot get along with other dogs. However, I refuse to believe that such a vast number of those in rescue centres could not live with another dog. We owe it to every dog to understand them better than we currently do. Recently, on a UK rescue centre's website, 303 dogs were looking for new homes. Only 61 of these were in the category 'could live with another dog'. That's just 20% – one in every five. So, 242 dogs will spend the rest of their life kept away from others of their species. Not what I would consider advantageous to any functional character. The following example was taken at random from this website, and the wording has been changed slightly to protect the dog in question:

> *'Rover [not a real name] can live in an adult-only home with someone home most of the day, and where he is the only dog. He would ideally like a home where he won't meet too many other dogs, as he finds this difficult. He will be a great new addition to his new family. The new owner needs to live within 30 minutes of the rescue centre.'*

I would absolutely *love* to adopt this dog! But I can't. I have other dogs, and I'm over 100 miles from the centre! Rover would benefit enormously from what I could offer him. I could help him

➤ discover who he truly is

➤ build his confidence around other dogs

➤ enable him to manage or conquer his current fears

➤ stay healthy with a species-appropriate diet and a chemical-free life.

After reading the advert, I believe that Rover's chances of finding a new home are not as good as they could be. It is heartbreaking. How long will this lovely dog languish in a kennel and be denied the chance of becoming what he could have been? Having run a rescue service myself for ten years, I am well aware that it can be incredibly tough to place dogs. I know that many centres are overworked and full, and that they are doing the best they can. But why limit an individual's chances of finding the right 'forever' home?

Suppose everyone involved in rehoming was conversant with an in-depth and working knowledge of functional characters and calming signals, the importance of feeding a species-appropriate diet, and the concept of dogs as an ecosystem. Add to that a deep understanding of how to take canine relationships forward for individual dogs and their new owners. Surely all of this would improve the way we serve the dog world than at present. In my own experience of getting a rescue dog, some rescue centre personnel have made it incredibly difficult to adopt. On a couple of occasions, I was talked at by staff who clearly had no practical experience of behaviour reformation – they just seemed intent on impressing me with all the scientific words and phrases they had learnt in academia!

I take my hat off to rescue centres, providing a bridge and hope for dogs to eventually find a loving and forever home. For some dogs, the sad reality is that this may never happen. However, by adding functional character to the assessment protocol, I feel it could be advantageous for so many.

Puppy purchase

Buying from a puppy farm or other deprived environment just to 'get them out of there' merely ensures that these lowlife 'breeders' stay in business. It also guarantees that the overworked breeding bitches will have to do it all over again when they next come into season. At my daycare facility, one of our regulars was one of these breeding bitches, until a rescue service stepped in. I'm glad to say that she now enjoys a marvellous lifestyle.

Deciding on a breed or breed mix is obviously the first step to choosing a puppy. If you would like to train your pet to become a helper dog and one of the tasks you have in mind is pulling you up from a sitting position, then choosing a small breed will not work for you. If you have a toddler or young children and would like a companion for them, a Great Dane might not be the best choice. It would be rare to see gundog people opt for anything other than a working breed and a working line. When there are children or family members with an allergy, then a poodle or poodle mix may be the way to go. However, there is no guarantee that these won't also create an allergic reaction.

So, you have decided on your breed or breed type, and you arrive at the breeder's home where their six-week-old puppies are contained in a playpen. Assuming there is at least one of each functional character in the litter, this is how they may appear:

GUIDE	At the back of the group, maybe behind another puppy. Watches the puppies, not the people. May look shy, but not scared. Is very aloof and may totally ignore you.
LONE INDIVIDUAL	Alone and usually on the periphery of the group. May look shy, but not scared. Continues to do its own thing.
DEFENDER	At the front of the group, ready to say 'hi' to you. Will be very noticeably bigger than the rest of the litter, and quite a bulky individual. Can also be clumsy.
OBSERVER	Maybe at the back with the Guide, or on the periphery of the group. Looks nervous or scared.
OVERSEER	The most excited puppy in the litter, like the ball in a pinball machine, and quite frantic with it!
PEACEKEEPER	Quietly saying 'hi' at the front of the group, maybe upside down. Can look more appeasing than the rest.
FOLLOWER	Maybe coming forward to say 'hi' or may still be asleep! They can also be large pups but might not be as bulky as Defenders.
HUNTER	Quite slim and maybe physically smaller than most in the litter. Very intent on watching movement above.
NANNY/GUARDIAN	This is an 'associate character' and is usually not seen in an individual before about 18 months of age.

If the breeder allows you to hold the puppies, this may help to give you an idea of their functional characters:

GUIDE	They observe all that goes on but are noticeably quiet. If you try to lay them on their backs on your lap, or snuggle with them, they will probably object by wriggling.
LONE INDIVIDUAL	As above.
DEFENDER	Very tactile; they may wriggle a lot as they would want to be off exploring somewhere, but equally will relax into the warmth and comfort of a lap!
OBSERVER	May object to being picked up and may 'freeze' as you go towards them. May look terrified while being held.
OVERSEER	If you can catch this 'live wire' to snuggle on your lap, they may nip a finger excessively, and hard!
PEACEKEEPER	May love snuggling on a lap, but may have one eye on the litter just in case they need to diffuse something.
FOLLOWER	Very tactile and would love snuggling on a lap. If they are comfortable, they can sleep anywhere!
HUNTER	May not engage with you fully as they have their own agenda: movement. They will watch something long after it stops moving and the other pups have fallen asleep, but if there is stillness, they will relax.

Functional character choice

Now it is time to consider which functional character or characters would be best suited to you, your current dog or social group. If this is your family's first dog, it's probably best to opt for a

Follower or Peacekeeper. For families that are more experienced, but still have young children, anything but an Overseer, Guide or Lone Individual may suit. A Defender may or may not work, depending on the children's ages and the chosen breed or breed mix. A Chihuahua Defender would be more manageable than a Spaniel, German Shepherd, Rottie or Staffie Defender, for example.

Your choice of functional character will depend on many things, for example:

➤ Is the puppy going to be purely a companion for you, or an older dog, etc.?

➤ Would you like a buddy for children to grow up with?

➤ Do you need a working pet, such as a helper dog?

➤ Will the puppy eventually become a qualified assistance dog through ADUK?

➤ Are you looking for a suitable individual for breed showing?

➤ Do you intend to take part in competition obedience or canine freestyle?

➤ Are you looking for a confident individual for agility, flyball or canicross?

We need to think deeply about our choice of functional character because not all of them are suited to certain roles, interactions, households, etc. Think of a professional person that you know – an accountant, for example. How well would that person be suited to a career as a bricklayer? The two jobs have vastly varied requirements and demand different temperaments and mental ability. Likewise, it may not be possible for you to achieve an enjoyable state of flyball competition with a Guide or an Observer. The Guide would be potentially hesitant due to the mix of unknown people, dogs and space, and the Observer may have a meltdown because of the proximity of high-energy individuals.

Functional characters to consider, and why	Functional characters to avoid, and why
A family that are first-time dog owners, who are active and have young children	
Follower – biddable, easy to train with food, happy to cuddle and nap a lot! **Peacekeeper** – ditto Follower	**Overseer** – needs a quieter home and lifestyle **Guide** – too aloof, doesn't like 'space invaders'! **Lone Individual** – ditto Guide **Observer** – too excitable for young children **Defender** – way too much to handle for first-timers!
A family that already have a dog, who are active with older children, and need a helper dog	
Follower and **Peacekeeper** – as above, although a more confident Follower may be required **Overseer** – might work for more patient owners. **Guide** – would learn the tasks quickly, but may be reticent in certain situations **Defender** – speedy learner with bags of energy but can settle and nap if required	**Observer** – may lack confidence for many helper dog tasks **Lone Individual** – may not be willing to learn a task if it involves close contact **Hunter** – may be worth a try but, equally, they may be too focused on movement elsewhere, rather than the task in hand!
A single person who needs to qualify their pet as an assistance dog	
Follower and **Peacekeeper** – as above, although a more confident Follower may be required **Guide** – would learn the tasks quickly, but may be reticent in certain situations **Defender** – speedy learner who may cope superbly with all the tasks of an assistance dog. **Hunter** – this may work if the individual is desensitised to movement from an early age	**Observer** – may lack confidence for many of the required tasks **Lone Individual** – may not be willing to undertake a task that involves an unknown person or dog. **Overseer** – may be challenging to obtain the desired level of self-control required for most exercises **Hunter** – reason as above
For breed showing	
Follower, Peacekeeper, Guide, Defender, Hunter – may all be able to cope with the requirements	**Observer** – may be traumatised at large events and would produce litters of nervous puppies **Lone Individual** – may not cope at busy shows **Overseer** – may be challenging to obtain the desired level of self-control required
For competition	
Choice of functional character here is a tough one to call. There are pros and cons for all of them when considering obedience, heelwork to music, canine freestyle, flyball, agility, canicross, etc. It may be best to refer to the individual functional character sections to get a better idea of what may work best.	

The table opposite gives you a rough guide regarding a potential choice as far as functional character is concerned. However, the caveat is that there are many other things to take into consideration – not least, the choice of breed. For example, a farm-bred Border Collie is not a good option unless they will be kept mentally stimulated most of the day, every day.

If you are considering adding another individual to your current social group, the following table may help you. It is based on the best-case scenario of the current dog being an adult of 3+ years and having no underlying behaviour problems, and the new dog being brought in as a young puppy less than 14 weeks of age.

Current Dog	Best Suited	Least Suited
Guide	Defender, Follower, Hunter, Peacekeeper, Lone Individual, or Guide of the opposite sex	Overseer, Observer, Guide of the same sex
Lone Individual	Guide – particularly of the opposite sex, Peacekeeper, Follower, Hunter, Lone Individual	Defender, Overseer, Observer
Defender	Guide of either sex, Peacekeeper, Observer, Follower, Hunter, Defender[1]	Lone Individual, Overseer
Observer	Defender, Peacekeeper, Follower, Hunter, Guide	Lone Individual, Overseer, Observer
Overseer[2]	Peacekeeper, Follower, Hunter, Observer	Guide, Defender, Overseer, Lone Individual
Peacekeeper	Guide, Defender, Hunter, Observer, Follower, Lone Individual, Peacekeeper	Overseer, with some exceptions
Follower	Guide, Defender, Hunter, Observer, Follower, Lone Individual, Peacekeeper	Overseer, with some exceptions
Hunter	Guide, Defender, Hunter, Observer, Follower, Lone Individual, Peacekeeper	Overseer, with some exceptions

[1] Two or more Defenders in one household may be rather tricky to handle!

[2] There is more chance of an owner being able to control the environment for an Overseer if they are the sole dog in the household.

The table above is just a guide. I am not suggesting for one minute that only certain characters are compatible. Indeed, group composition is often challenging to get right as all dogs are individual. As Dr Isla Fishburn says, 'Group dynamics may mean that 2+ dogs may naturally oppose one another. A social animal does not mean social to all.'

You may have noticed that I have listed an Overseer to be least suited to all other characters. It is possible, of course, for Overseers to complement and live peacefully with other functional characters. However, I would say this is only the case with an experienced home, or where someone had existing knowledge of the Overseer, what to expect, and how to support them and their group.

Many things need to be considered to get the best affinity between individuals and a group. We should aim to create harmony and safety, not conflict and discord within our multi-dog homes. Watching the dogs at my daycare facility, we see them naturally gravitate into smaller groups and towards compatible individuals. The more dogs we have in, the more harmony we see – probably because a big group affords more choice, whereas a smaller group has only a small selection of potential 'chums'.

It is super interesting that, on more than one occasion, an owner has told us that if 'dog X' is at daycare on a particular day, they would prefer their dog not to come. The reason is that 'dog X' is reactive when they meet out on a walk. At daycare, we have never had a problem between the two individuals in question. The reason for this is that conflict, and coexistence, vary from location to location, and both can be affected by temporary group composition, such as daycare and dog parks, etc. Also, the reaction of the owner or other person nearby, after an event between dogs, can affect the relationship between the dogs in that place the next time they meet.

Here is an example from my own group on how a different location can affect them. My male Lone Individual is more than happy to play chase with my female Defender when we are out, but does not want her anywhere near him once we are back at the van or at home. He enjoys her strength, in terms of confident exploring and chasing around the forest while out, but he is intimidated by that same strength in more confined surroundings. Also, as a Lone Individual, he has a reasonably large personal space bubble. He is generally grumpy with any dog or person that may look as though they will get too close. His 'bestie' is a Peacekeeper at daycare. They have known each other since she was a few months old and she is the only one he will play with, irrespective of location.

Living in harmony with multiple dogs is extremely rewarding but can be challenging at times. Ditto if you are a professional working with groups of dogs. However, what has made both my job and my life with multiple dogs infinitely easier is learning about functional characters. It is certainly a far cry from the 1980s, when my career as a dog trainer had just started, and I had a group of 11 dogs. The group consisted of one Dobermann, one crossbreed (Labrador/German pointer), and nine Rottweilers. I also ran a rescue service for Rotties, so there were always new dogs coming and going. All the dogs lived indoors as my house was large and we had over an acre of garden. When I think back, I wonder how on earth it all worked, but it did.

I learned early on in my career that most behaviour problems are not fixed by a visit to the vet. Dogs need understanding, not drugs, although I appreciate that there may be times when pills and potions are required to help get remedial work underway. By 'understanding', I do not mean fluffy stuff such as treating dogs like little children or memorising all the fancy behaviour terms used by academics in behavioural science. I simply mean that the more familiar we are with our four-legged companions – how they tick, why they do what they do and act the way they act – the better. I believe we should be a 'Guide' to our dogs, providing them with a 'go-to' person, thus creating stability within a social group. Our households do not need to be run like dictatorships – dogs should be given choices. For example, if you have a Guide and are out on a walk, sometimes allow them to choose which way to go or which track to take – this is an excellent tip I picked up from Dr Isla Fishburn, and it works a treat!

Remember that food source is crucial if you have a group. Once inside, the scent of food exudes through the skin and coat. In turn, this affects the interactions and communication between individuals. An example would be to imagine two dogs at daycare – a Follower whose breakfast was chicken wings, and a Guide who had only consumed tripe. Because the wings give the Follower a more pungent scent, he may hide somewhere, avoid the Guide, or not want to empty, in an effort not to 'advertise' his scent.

Scent is an integral part of canine communication – it is how dogs 'see' the world, and has a bearing on how they interact with each other. Neutering (de-sexing) removes a dog's ability, via scent, to communicate that it is capable of reproducing. Sexual status can be one of the causes of same-gender tiffs. These have the potential to develop into physical injury if the energy building between them is not observed soon enough and redirected. At my daycare facility, we once saw a five-year-old neutered female Guide doing rather intense 'speed and direction' to an adolescent female Follower. Speed and direction is when one individual 'controls' the speed and direction of another to suppress and communicate differences between them. However, after the Follower was spayed, things settled down very well between them. Now they offer each other some lovely calming signals and have even been seen napping on the same sofa! Remember also that exercising increases adrenaline, which changes the scent of a dog.

It is also essential to understand that neutering does not solve all the issues dogs of both sexes may have around other dogs, or people. If you have an un-neutered male Follower and a neutered male Guide, be aware that your Guide may likely give the Follower a hard time. Certainly, this may include speed and direction outside, but may also involve other forms of 'control' indoors. For example, the Guide may sit in a doorway to prevent the Follower from entering or leaving the room.

In the dog world, just as in wolves, age is knowledge, which is why it is good to try and have four or five years between dogs. Obviously, with large groups, it may not be possible to have this kind of age difference. In her online Canine Wellness Course, Dr Isla Fishburn tells us, 'We do need to be aware of the potential issues that can arise due to small gaps in age disparity. If more significant age gaps are not possible, consider how changing breeds could help.' So, if you have an adolescent terrier (a dog bred to flush out prey), they would be complemented by any of the retrieving breeds, or a crossbreed with retriever in it.

If your current dog is slightly reactive to other dogs and you are considering another dog, choose one of the opposite sex to your current one. However, in the first instance, you may need to discover the reason for the reactivity. If your pet is *highly* reactive to other dogs, I would advise you to seek professional advice as soon as possible. Once a behaviour problem becomes ingrained, it can be stressful and time consuming to remedy. Seek out a qualified dog behaviour expert and someone who understands functional characters if possible. Please, please research potential trainers – there are still many non-positive reinforcement professionals out there. A trainer in a different area to where I am located used a shock collar on a dog that used to come to my daycare facility. The dog was attending a three-week board and train programme. When the dog returned to daycare, we noticed that it was exceptionally subdued, but could not work out why. I was later told by someone who knew the whole sorry saga that the dog had been 'trained' using a shock collar. A few months later, the dog was rehomed – not via a rescue centre, but to the shock collar trainer! My heart still breaks for that lovely dog whose only 'issues' were breed predispositions, and a lack of location-specific training.

Having unpeeled another layer to our dogs that we didn't even know existed, we have a little more insight into them. And now that we know more about how to choose our next dog, and *why* we're choosing that particular character, will it make us more selective of the puppy or adult dog we bring home? Yes, absolutely! But isn't that what we want? Surely, to understand our pets at a much deeper level is beneficial to both species? And, ending up with a character that complements our current dog or group will, in the long run, save a lot of heartache in the future. I know of some breeders who are already helpfully pairing up their pups with new owners and their lifestyle using their new knowledge of functional characters.

With an increased working knowledge of functional characters, calming signals and dogs as an ecosystem, we can go some way to preventing so many unwanted and abandoned souls.

13 Food, Cancer & Chemicals

'The food you eat can either be the safest and most powerful form of medicine, or the slowest form of poison'.

− ANN WIGMORE

Species-appropriate diet

In the section on 'Diet and digestion' in Chapter 2, we explored why our view of a dog's functional character can be distorted by what we feed them. To understand *why* food has such a significant bearing on behaviour, take a quick look at the three 'systems' inside your dog:

➤ immune

➤ digestive

➤ nervous.

All three are inextricably linked, so what goes into the digestive system also affects the nervous system but, more significantly, the immune system.

Processed pet food and treats contain many poor-quality ingredients that not only severely affect the health of our beloved dogs, but also cause behaviours that potentially 'mask' a dog's functional character.

Processed dog food contains low-grade ingredients, and the manufacturing process changes the molecular structure of these ingredients. When this all reaches the dog's gut, it does not recognise it as 'food', and the dog is changed at a cellular level. This change happens because 90 per cent of serotonin production occurs in the gut, and serotonin is the chemical that stabilises mood. Since mood affects emotions, we can now see the link between what we feed our pets and their emotions. In essence, a dog's behaviour is affected by their diet.

Feeding a species-appropriate diet is key to a dog's health and wellbeing, which starts on the inside as we have seen. Also, what we feed determines not only behaviour and health, but also what the dog's poo is like! Dogs fed on processed food produce a lot of poo, which can be runny and foul smelling – not great for a dog's anal glands, our pockets or the environment, as it means we use more poo bags!

'Dogs have the highest rate of cancer than any other animal on the planet. 1 in 1.65 will die of it.'

– Rodney Habib, Natural Dog Conference, Birmingham, December 2015

Rodney Habib is a Canadian blogger and founder of the largest pet health page on Facebook – Planet Paws. As of October 2020, he has nearly 3.5 million followers. Often called 'the Jamie Oliver of pet health', Rodney campaigns to eliminate cancer from the dog world. If you've not yet seen his excellent TEDx talk, please check it out at www.rodneyhabib.com/rodney-habib-tedx and for further information, you can visit www.planetpaws.ca.

You may still be wondering why we should feed our dogs a species-appropriate diet. That is understandable if you have never had the opportunity to research processed dog food. Also, there are still so many qualified professionals not following the science that is out there. Until 2005 I believed *everything* my vet told me about feeding and vaccinating my dogs. In 2009, I lost my best obedience and heelwork to music Rottweiler after he was diagnosed with an enlarged heart. I had already started to research the ingredients in processed dog food when I lost him, but then I turned my attention to annual vaccinations and the other chemicals prescribed by my vet for regular 'treatment'. The Rottweiler's story is for another time, and information on vaccinations is at the end of this chapter.

Some of the information from my research, and countless courses attended over the past 15-20 years, is in this book. The rest will follow in subsequent books! During my research into food ingredients, I also looked at how and why dogs eat the way they do.

The jaws of all canids are intended for a more carnivorous diet because:

➤ their jaws only go up and down

➤ their teeth are designed for chopping, not chewing.

Human jaws can move sideways *and* up/down because the jaw is hinged above the level of the teeth. This amount of movement is ideal for chewing and grinding food and starting the digestive process. However, canid jaws have their hinge at the same level as the teeth, which is beneficial for up/down, scissor-like movements, and holding on to wriggling and writhing prey, but does not allow for any sideways movement. Their eating action is crush-crunch-swallow, and the digestive system is designed to process chunks of food, rather than dealing with it in a ground-up form. Even raw bone can be dealt with by the digestive system because the acid level in a natural-fed dog's gut is exceptionally high. A dog's digestive process starts in the gut, as opposed to a human's, which begins in the mouth.

www.vivahealth.org.uk/wheat-eaters-or-meat-eaters/jaw-motion-and-chewing-mastication

Dentition also is quite different between canids and humans. We have large molars designed for chewing and grinding plant matter, but dogs are equipped with larger, self-sharpening pairs of teeth. These teeth, called carnassials, are towards the back of their jaw and are ideal for shredding meat.

Inside a canid, the digestive tract is much shorter than that of a human. Our longer digestive tract provides a larger surface area for food to be digested, as well as more time for plant matter to be digested. Grains take more time to digest than meat and so we can instantly understand why dogs:

➤ are not able to easily digest grains

➤ are designed for a meat and bones diet

➤ suffer from many health issues on a processed diet.

Although dogs are primarily carnivores, they do forage for plants and berries. If living outside a domestic environment, they would scavenge for anything they could find. Indeed, just like our Palaeolithic ancestors, different foods would be eaten as the seasons changed. However, despite thousands of years of domestication, a dog *has not* evolved physically to consume or digest grain or processed food.

'Why are we not feeding what a dog has spent 4.2 million years evolving to eat?'

– Dr Nick Thompson, Natural Raw Feeding Seminar, Bradford, February 2020

These days it is widely understood that a dog's immune system resides in the gastrointestinal tract (the gut). In her Complete Canine Wellness course, Dr Isla Fishburn says, 'diet is important because the food affects the microbiome in the digestive tract, which supports the immune system.' To avoid the chronic inflammation that can occur throughout the body, caused by the lamentable nutrition in processed pet food, it is essential to feed our pets a natural, fresh food diet.

A dog's body is unable to recognise processed food as a food source. This is because the ingredients have gone through immense changes during the manufacturing process to arrive at the finished product – bag upon bag of hard feed that always looks and tastes the same.

The ingredients in processed dog food are cooked at really high temperatures, and often re-cooked as many as four times. All this changes the metabolics of the food, rendering it unrecognisable once inside the dog's gut. Because the food is not recognised as such, a dog's immune system is triggered at each meal – just as it is every time we vaccinate them. Over-stimulation of the immune system eventually causes it to attack 'self', which can trigger any of the numerous autoimmune diseases – cancer being one.

When food is fried, toasted or roasted, it turns brown to a lesser or greater degree, depending on the cooking time. This changing of colour is known as a Maillard reaction and is caused by amino acid reacting with reducing sugar. It is similar to, but not the same as, caramelisation. The cooking process changes the way the original ingredients look, smell and taste. Some examples of Maillard reactions are the colour of coffee, black lines on a barbequed steak, biscuits and burnt toast.

The extreme cooking temperatures used in the manufacturing of dry dog food produce some acrylamides through the Maillard reaction. Acrylamide levels in food vary. They are also present in tobacco smoke, and some are used to make copolymers. Exposure to acrylamides has been suggested to increase the risk of cancer. References:

➤ www.differencebetween.com/difference-between-maillard-reaction-and-caramelization

➤ www.dartagnan.com/caramelization-vs-browning.html

➤ www.vedantu.com/chemistry/maillard-reaction

➤ www.pyrolysisplant.com/what-is-pyrolysis

➤ www.cancer.gov/about-cancer-prevention/risk/diet/acrylamide-fact-sheet

➤ www.cancer.org/cancer/cancer-causes/acrylamide.html

Dr Brendan Clarke is the head vet at Towerwood Vets in Leeds, and the President of the Raw Feeding Veterinary Society. In an interview with Bella & Duke's nutritionist, Rowan Sanderson, Dr Clarke said:

> 'When protein goes through high heat, the structure of the protein changes. Protein products subjected to high heat can end up becoming carcinogens, possibly irritate the gut lining via inflammation, and lead to allergies involving gastric upset or skin problems.'

Between 1985 and 2013, I had the privilege of sharing my life with a total of 40 Rottweilers. Thirty-three of them died of cancer. All were fed on processed dry dog food, as suggested by whatever vet I had at the time. They were aged between three and nine years old when I had to have them put to sleep. At the time, I did not think there might be a connection between their deaths and their food, because I was aware that Rottweilers are more prone to bone cancer than almost any other breed. However, when I started to research dog food ingredients, I began to understand why I had lost more than 80 per cent of my beloved Rotties to cancer.

For years, I berated myself and asked several vets questions about why I had lost so many of my dogs at such a young age. None of them suggested that it had anything to do with diet, or any of the chemicals they were happy to prescribe month after month, year after year. And so, for a while, I kept feeding the trash they peddled and kept following their advice on vaccinations, and flea and worm treatments.

Some dog world professionals say that dogs are far removed from their ancestor – the wolf. They also tell us that dogs have 'evolved over the past 100 years to eat and easily digest biscuit-type food made from grains'. However, there is an immense amount of evidence from myriad specialists, including veterinarians who specialise in canine diet and behaviour, to suggest otherwise. For example:

'Dogs are in the genus 'Canis' which is over 10 million years old – hence they are an indigenous canine' and *'A body that is not fed*

correctly is unable to function effectively, communicate and repair at a cellular level – the building blocks that make life.'

> – Dr Isla Fishburn BSc (Zoology and MBiolSci), PhD
> (Conservation Biology), https://kachinacanine.com/

'The theory behind raw food is that dogs and cats have evolved to eat raw food and have been eating it since their ancestor crawled out of the oceans. Logically, if you feed a diet that is readily recognised, efficiently digested and easily assimilated by the mammalian body, you will get less antagonism between food and teeth, food and gut, food and the immune system.'

> – Dr Nick Thompson BSc (Hons) Path Sci, BVM&S,
> VetMFHom., MRCVS, https://holisticvet.co.uk/index.php/articles/

'After a doctorate studying the effects of nutrition on the behaviour and gut morphology of animals, five years with guide dogs as a trainer and supervisor, some success on Dragons' Den with the finest raw dog food company and the last few years both writing and speaking on canine nutrition and health, I can say with some confidence that the pet food and drug industry cares not a jot for the health of your pet.'

> – Dr Conor Brady (zoologist and independent animal
> nutritionist), https://dogsfirst.ie/what-is-the-best-80-20-dog-
> food-in-uk/

Bella & Duke's Podcast 49 is an excellent introduction to Dr Brady: www.bellaandduke.com/podcast/why-you-should-not-cook-meat-for-your-dogpodcast-49

*'Pets need unadulterated, fresh, whole foods that are moisture dense. They **do not** need grains, fillers, artificial preservatives, colours, additives, chemicals, by-products or processed foods. Although animals can eat some processed foods, they aren't designed to consume a lifetime of dry or canned diets.'*

> – Dr Karen Becker DVM, www.youtube.com/watch?v=
> Qx2YllpF4cc, https://healthypets.mercola.com/sites/
> healthypets/archive/2017/05/31/pet-raw-food-diet.aspx

Dr W Jean Dodds DVM has been a practising veterinarian since 1964 and is widely acknowledged as a world leader in canine vaccination protocols and healthy foods for dogs.

www.hemopet.org/education/w-jean-dodds

With kind permission from Dr Jean Dodds, here is an excerpt from her book *Canine Nutrigenomics*, which was co-written with Diana Laverdure.

> *'Have you ever wondered why the topic of raw diets generates such passionate opinions, regardless of which side people are on? Maybe it is because so many well-intentioned mainstream veterinarians are vehemently opposed to feeding raw. These professionals have been warned against raw diets since veterinary school by – guess who? – nutrition spokespeople who represent large commercial pet food producers! Suitably fearful, they pass this fear along to their clients. Some of these veterinarians even refuse to treat dogs who consume raw meats.'*

Other veterinary supporters of healthy dogs are:

➤ Dr Marty Goldstein DVM, author of *The Nature of Animal Healing*

➤ Dr Susanna McIntyre BSc, MRCVS, founder of the British Veterinary Dental Association in 1988 (see www.petplusvet.com/about).

As they have descended through thousands of years of domestication, dogs' appearance has altered many times. Their digestive system has not. I take this as confirmation that they should be fed a species-specific diet, not the overcooked, nutritionally deficient kibble peddled by so many professionals. As we all know – diet is the key to health.

There is no getting away from the fact that diet has a bearing on immune efficiency, irrespective of chemical vaccinations. Therefore the food a dog consumes is hugely important not just for its health and wellbeing, but also for its immune function.

Emotion is the driving force of all dog behaviour, and emotions can be affected by what a dog eats. Functional character also impacts the behaviours that result from a dog's emotions. In other words, what we feed our dogs helps determine how they behave and react in their environment, in any given situation. Some functional characters are more reactive by nature than others. Feed these characters on processed food and their reactivity may be exacerbated. When I say 'reactive', I mean in the context of sensitive or fearful, not aggressive.

Here is another excellent excerpt from the Bella & Duke interview with Dr Brendan Clarke:

'When proteins are hydrolysed through cooking, they may provoke behavioural issues in dogs by creating a surge of excitatory neurotransmitters. Perhaps this could be due to an end product that can only be used for energy but cannot be used for the building blocks the body needs.

'On the other hand, dogs seemingly become calmer and more focused after switching to a raw diet. Food that enhances the microbiome and health of your animal, naturally gives them focused, boundless energy that they can turn off when not needed, like when they are at home.'

Much of my work as a behaviourist involves helping owners with highly reactive dogs. In the past ten years alone, I have seen a significant percentage of them change for the better once their diet was switched to raw. A few did not make such a stunning transformation. I believe this was because they were still fed myriad processed dog treats or changed back to a processed diet after being criticised by their vet. Other dogs that did not make much progress were the ones still having veterinary prescribed 'treatments'. These include dental chews, monthly worm and flea treatments, and other chemicals that can overwhelm a dog's body, such as annual vaccinations.

Insecticides and vaccination

Just as you would use the insecticides on your garden plants and shrubs to rid them of bugs, many veterinarians now insist we do the same with our pets.

Bravecto is the brand name for Fluralaner, the active ingredient in this product, manufactured by Merck & Co Incorporated – known as MSD outside North America. Fluralaner (carbamoyl benzamide phenyl isoxazoline) is part of the isoxazoline drug class of insecticides. This group of drugs was launched in the USA in 2014 and included sarolaner, afoxolaner and lotilaner.

➤ https://files.brief.vet/2018-03/PTB_TS_Isoxazolines.pdf

➤ https://vcahospitals.com/know-your-pet/fluralaner

➤ www.acs.org/content/acs/en/molecule-of-the-week/archive/f/fluralaner.html

➤ https://us.bravecto.com

➤ www.ema.europa.eu/en/documents/mrl-report/fluralaner-poultry-european-public-maximum-residue-limit-assessment-report-epmar-cvmp_en.pdf

Fluralaner is a systemic insecticide that, once ingested, is transported around a dog's body via the blood. When an insect bites and feeds on the dog's blood, the chemical enters its body and the insect is killed. Death is caused by uncontrolled activity in the nervous system. So, our dogs are not protected from insect bites as they must still get bitten by the flea or tick for the parasite to die! I wonder how many dog owners have stopped to think about what damage the insecticide is doing to their dog's body.

Bravecto.com advises us that *'Fluralaner is a member of the isoxazoline class. This class has been associated with neurologic adverse reactions including tremors, ataxia* [damage to the brain, spinal cord or other nerves], *and seizures'.* Bravecto's 'Important Safety Information' discloses *'Seizures have been reported in dogs receiving isoxazoline class drugs, even in dogs without a history of seizures.'*

For more information on this subject see https://isbravectosafe.com/bravectotruefacts.htm

So, what are the alternatives to insecticides for treating parasites? The table below shows a selection of products from companies that only produce natural products.

Parasite	Product	Manufacturer	Notes
Fleas, ticks	Nature's Bounty	Hedgerow Hounds	Changes the taste of the blood to the bugs
Fleas, ticks, worms and bedbugs	Diatomaceous Earth	Natural Supplies	Externally, kills by dehydrating the bugs, and internally it detoxes the digestive system
Fleas, ticks, worms, flies and mosquitos	Insect Defence Spray	Dermadog	An essential oil blend that deodorises a dog to prevent bugs
Fleas, ticks	Cedarcide spray	Cedarcide.com – UK distributor is naturalenzymes.co.uk	Natural cedar oil that leaches the moisture from the bugs
Fleas, ticks, worms, mites and bedbugs	All-in-One Preventer	Hands and Paws	Natural ingredients absorbed around the dog's system to repel bugs and clean out any worms
Fleas, ticks	Neem Shield Spray	Serendipity Herbals aka theneemteam.co.uk	Natural ingredients that deter bugs and give your dog's coat a good sheen

It is my firm belief that annual vaccinations, aided by a processed food diet, killed most of the Rottweilers I owned. During my initial research into over-vaccination, or what many vets call 'annual vaccinations' and see as totally necessary, I read these excellent books:

What Vets Don't Tell You about Vaccines by Catherine O'Driscoll. Here are a couple of the summary points that Catherine makes at the end of her chapters:

➤ 'Notable immunologists tell us that immunity to a virus persists for years, or for life, and annual vaccination is not necessary.'

➤ 'Vaccines do not confer guaranteed protection.'

The Nature of Animal Healing by Dr Marty Goldstein DVM:

> *'Cancer, after all, simply doesn't occur in hosts with strong immune systems. Vaccines, given as copiously as they are to pets, stress the immune system; the pets get cancer; the vaccines cause cancer. Call it a corollary to classic Aristotelian logic: If A creates B and B creates C, then A creates C.'*

Dr Ronald Schultz PhD is professor and chair of the Department of Pathobiological Sciences at the University of Wisconsin-Madison School of Veterinary Medicine and has more than 40 years' experience in the field of immunology. This is a very interesting article he wrote back in 2003: https://news.wisc.edu/schultz-dog-vaccines-may-not-be-necessary/

Did you know that thimerosal is the preservative in your dog's vaccine (and in human vaccines, for that matter) and that it contains high levels of mercury? See Robert F. Kennedy's book *Thimerosal: Let the Science Speak*.

Even the World Small Animal Veterinary Association (WSAVA) states that a vaccination lasts for three years. So, instead of wading in with vaccinations, why don't we check the immune levels first with a titre test? This is a simple blood test that checks an individual's antibody response to the core vaccines, preventing over-vaccination or under-vaccination. More information can be found here: www.vaccicheck.com

Before I put anything inside my dogs, I question it. What is it? Where does it come from? Why am I giving it to them? What benefit will they derive from it? Will it harm them? Do they really need it? I will no longer be bullied or brainwashed by those who claim to have my dogs' best interests, and health, at heart.

And finally, here is what I think is probably the best book you will ever buy: *Feeding Dogs Dry Or Raw? The Science behind the Debate* by Dr Conor Brady. Yes, it is huge (548 pages), but it is written in such a way as to be an easy read for beginners and boffins alike. Enjoy!

I wish you and your dogs a long, happy, and healthy life.

Acknowledgements

This book would not have been possible without the amazing help and support of so many people, and dogs.

I would like to thank:

...my awesome team at CentreBarks, whose reliability, steadfast support and friendship are more appreciated than they can ever know.

...Julie Doyle and Kayleigh Maltby, whose enthusiasm and obsession with functional characters spurred me on to write a book on the subject.

...Dr Isla Fishburn, whose friendship and guidance, knowledge and wisdom, and several learning sessions at various eateries prior to the pandemic, helped make this book a reality.

...Michael Heppell, whose personal help and Write That Book Masterclass kept me on track and gave me a calm and friendly place in which to learn and grow.

...to Jennifer Flint for her brilliant suggestion on the change of title – I look forward to seeing your egg hatch!

...everyone who attended a functional character workshop for allowing me to learn from your dogs.

...Vicky Fraser for her amazing book *How The Hell Do I Write A Book?* and for her help during the pre-writing process.

... the most awesome vet on the planet, Dr W Jean Dodds, for her help with the Food, Cancer & Chemicals chapter.

...my beta readers – Dr W Jean Dodds, Susanne Excell, Julie Doyle, Rachel Chattle, Ross McCarthy and Dr Isla Fishburn.

...all the dogs, particularly the reactive ones, that have walked life's path with me, encouraging me to learn a little more about their species every day – you were excellent teachers.

...my sister Cindy Stendera for her encouragement and patient listening during the stressful moments.

...my Tuesday night training group for allowing me to obsess about this subject during our training classes, and for their excellent training abilities with their dogs.

...all the members of my private Facebook group for their mutual enthusiasm, interest and understanding of functional characters, and their support of this book during the writing process.

...everyone at Flying Squad Books who had a hand in the production of this book – thank you so much for your assistance throughout.

...my current dogs KD, Wizzi and Ava for your patience while I toiled away at the computer for hours on end – your company, and unconditional love is priceless.

And for anyone I have forgotten, I would like to thank you too.

Hopefully, this book has given you an excellent insight into canine functional characters, and allowed you to see your dogs in a different light than before. I also hope that you now have enough information to help you choose your next dog so that it complements your lifestyle and your current canine group.

At the time of writing, I am planning to roll out our Beyond the Breed Functional Character workshops to all parts of the UK, so that many more people can enjoy seeing the practical side of this knowledge.

We look forward to seeing you very soon.

TO BOOK A WORKSHOP FOR YOUR AREA, DOG CLUB OR BUSINESS:

➤ Please ring Heather on 075555 06456 or email beyondthebreedbook@gmail.com

➤ For book orders, please visit www.beyondthebreed.co.uk or email the above address.

"The world would be a nicer place if everyone had the ability to love as unconditionally as a dog.'

– M.K. CLINTON

Printed in Great Britain
by Amazon

72415468R10068